# Building Character Through Quran (and Sunnah)

This course seeks a much-needed paradigm shift and strikes a much-needed balance between the rights of Allah and those of fellow human beings. A deep dive into the Quran and the life of Prophet Muhammad for the gems they offer on character building. Examples are included of various human virtues and how Allah and the Prophet Muhammad encourage Muslims to incorporate them into their character.

**Ghamidi Center
of Islamic Learning**

www.ghamidi.org   AN INITIATIVE OF AL-MAWRID US.

Publisher: Ghamidi Center of Islamic Learning - Al-Mawrid US
ISBN: 978-1-966600-28-2

Address: 3620 N Josey Ln, Suite 230 Carrollton, TX 75007
Website: www.ghamidicenter.com
Email: info@ghamidi.org

# Chapter 1

# Introduction to the Course

This chapter introduces the course and its objectives.

# Introduction

- This course is the first concrete step toward discussing in depth the topics at the core of this entire Sunday School program, i.e., developing a strong Islamic moral character.
- Extensive research on character development shows that the initial years are critical in children's moral and emotional development.
- Traditionally, Muslim children are taught to focus only on performing the worship rituals to attain inner purity, which tilts the balance towards the rights of Allah, our God, while completely neglecting the rights of fellow human beings.
- This course aims to effect a much-needed paradigm shift and to balance Allah's rights with those of fellow human beings. It aims to achieve a "balanced" personality that avoids extremes, combining spiritual devotion with active, ethical engagement in society.
- We will dive deep into the Quran and Sunnah to explore the gems they offer for character building. We will learn how the Quran shapes a strong Muslim character. Examples from the Quran and Sunnah will be included on various human virtues and how Allah SWT and Prophet Muhammad encourage Muslims to incorporate these virtues into their character.
- In other words, we will explore what kind of believer God wants to see within us.

## Course Objectives

At the end of this course, the students will be able to:

- Describe what kind of character Allah wants from them.
- Examine their character and compare it with what they have learned.
- Improve their interaction and relationship with people around them.
- Identify situations where they can make a difference due to moral behavior.

## Entering the world of the Quran (L4 - L6)

- This course is the first of the three courses that concentrate on the Quran. In L5 and L6, the students will study the Quran in depth.

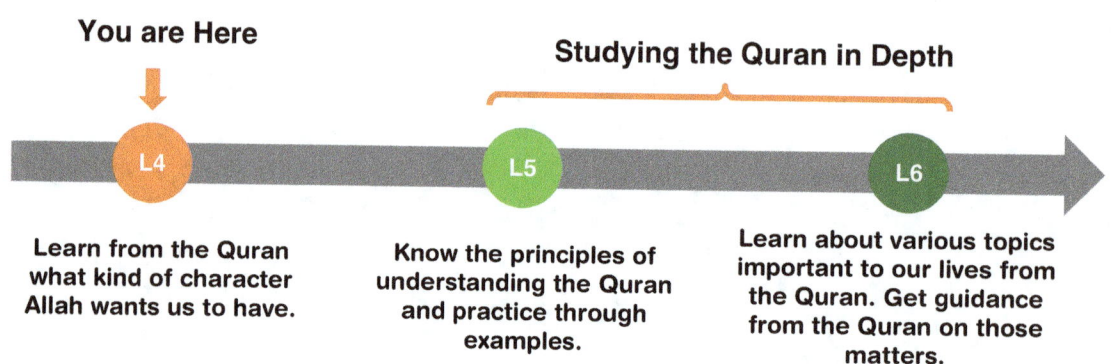

Consider this scenario. Your neighbor, John Doe, is a non-Muslim. He is a very nice guy. He cares for his family and neighbors and is very kind to everyone.

The question is, without knowing the Quran and Prophet Muhammad, how is it even possible that John Doe is such a good human being?

# Building character through the Quran

## Good character

- In Islam, great emphasis is placed on cultivating an excellent human character, also called "**Husnul Khuluq**".
- God inspired fundamental morality at the time of our creation.
- The Quran guides us in building that character on top of fundamental morality.
- A good character demonstrates moral behavior.
- Prophet Muhammad was sent to perfect the character of a Muslim, and he has demonstrated to us well how to achieve that.
- Perfecting character was so important for him that he considered it the sole reason for his being sent as a Prophet. He is reported to have said in one of the hadith:

بُعِثْتُ لِأُتَمِّمَ حُسْنَ الْأَخْلَاقِ

I have been sent to perfect good moral character. (Hadith Al-Muwatta 1614)

## The Sources

- For a Muslim, there are two main sources for building character and adopting a moral life: the Quran and the life of Prophet Muhammad. Both sources are based on human nature.
- That means every instruction in the Quran and the teachings of Prophet Muhammad regarding moral behavior is already rooted in our nature. These two are only perfecting it and taking it to the next level. The Quran stated that fact in verses 33:21 and 17:9.

**Human Nature (Al-Fitrah) - The Foundation**

إِنَّ هٰذَا الْقُرْآنَ يَهْدِى لِلَّتِى هِىَ أَقْوَمُ

In reality, this Quran shows the way, which is **absolutely straight.** (17:9)

لَقَدْ كَانَ لَكُمْ فِى رَسُولِ اللّٰهِ أُسْوَةٌ حَسَنَةٌ

The Messenger of God is the **best example** for you. (33:21)

# The significance of good character in Islam

- Allah said in the Quran about Prophet Muhammad while addressing him:

وَإِنَّكَ لَعَلَىٰ خُلُقٍ عَظِيمٍ

  And indeed, (O Muhammad), you are of a great moral character. (Quran 68:4)

- Prophet Muhammad said in one of the famous hadith:

  "Nothing will be heavier on the Day of Judgment in the scale of the believer than good character. (Hadith Tirmidhi: 626)"

- After faith, the second most important requirement of religion is the perfection of morals, or simply the cultivation of good character.

- We are required to follow our Prophet Muhammad, who was a living example of the highest moral character.

- It brings God's blessings to a person's life, to the family, to society, to the country, and to the world.

- Paying attention to good character improves our interactions and relationships with people around us. It helps us in situations where we can make a difference due to our good character.

- It is the source of all righteous/good deeds. It will help us the most to be successful on the day of judgment.

- We are required to purify (an act of cleaning) our behavior towards God and fellow human beings, and building our character plays a key role in achieving that goal.

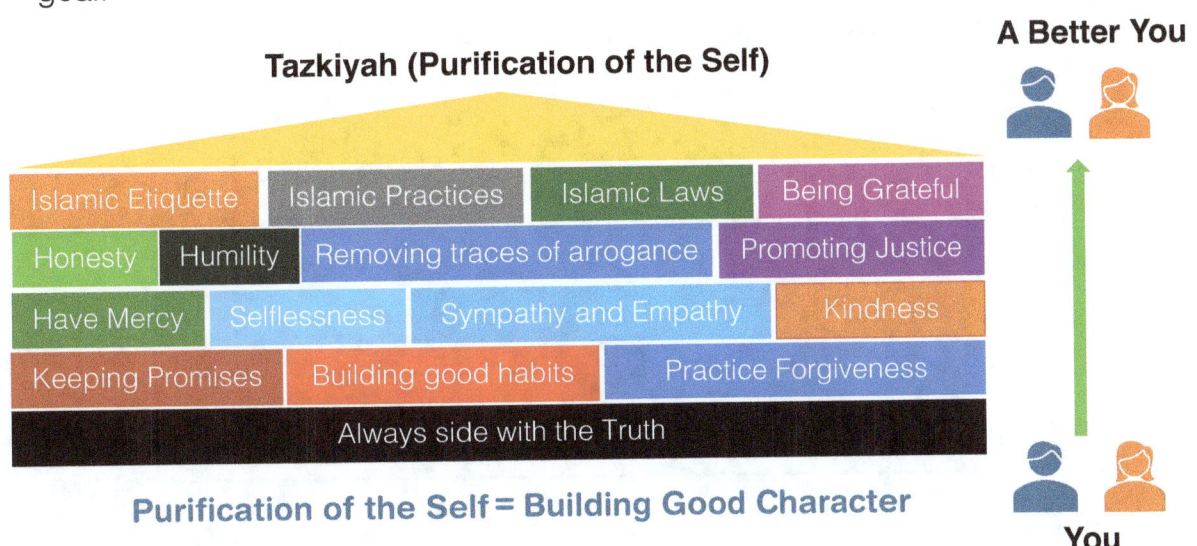

## Good character and religion

- Good character and religion are not two separate things; they are the same thing. One of the greatest scholars of Islam, Ibn Al-Qayyam, said beautifully:

> "Religion itself means good character, so whoever beats you in good character has beaten you in religion."

## How to benefit from this course?

✓ Identify one or two habits or traits/qualities of yours that are good. You want to continue to have, and even improve them.

✓ Identify one or two habits or behaviors of yours that you think are not good, and you want to get rid of them.

✓ Practice what you learn from this course – building new traits or improving on them and getting rid of old ones is a slow process and requires a lot of practice and patience.

✓ Start practicing from your home – most people do not practice good manners in their homes.

✓ Self-assess your day every day for 5 minutes before you go to sleep.

## Supplications from the Quran and the Prophet's Best Example

- Allah and Prophet Muhammad have taught us the following supplications. Here, knowledge refers to the knowledge of religion and good and evil.

رَّبِّ زِدْنِي عِلْمًا

O my Lord, increase me in knowledge. (Quran 20:114)

اللَّهُمَّ إِنِّي أَعُوذُ بِكَ مِنْ مُنْكَرَاتِ الْأَخْلَاقِ وَالْأَعْمَالِ وَالْأَهْوَاءِ

O Allah, I seek refuge in You from evil morals, evil actions, and evil desires. (Hadith Tirmidhi: 3591)

Discuss what practical steps you can take to benefit from this course.

# Important notes

- Throughout the course, the words God and Allah are used interchangeably.
- For brevity and editing, the salutations for the Prophet Muhammad, PEACE BE UPON HIM, are not repeated. But it is highly encouraged that whenever we say or read his name, we send him salutations.

# Class instructions

- You are required to attend all classes unless you have a valid reason to skip.
- Please send a note (or ask your parents) to your teacher on Google Classroom if you will skip a session.
- Attendance will be taken at the beginning of every class. Arriving in class 5 minutes after the start will be counted as tardy.
- Three (3) tardies will be counted as one absence.
- Attendance will be counted toward your final assessment.
- Every student will be assessed via:
  - Participation in the class
  - Multiple Quizzes
  - Assignments
  - Semester Exam
  - End-of-Year Exam

# Chapter 2

# Ethics and Morality

This chapter covers the basics of ethics and morality, their relationship to religion, and, specifically, to Islam.

# Ethics, Morality and Religion

- Both Ethics and Morality concern good and evil, or right and wrong, and are used interchangeably, but there is a clear distinction between the two.

## Ethics

Standards and principles imposed by an external entity, group, society, or religion.

## Morality

One's inner sense of right and wrong and external conduct within a society.

- Like the faculty of seeing and hearing, Allah has blessed humans with a faculty that distinguishes right from wrong. In other words, human beings are moral beings.
- In addition to the innate moral sense given to human beings, Allah provided ethics (codes of conduct) through messengers and books to guide individuals' morals.

The ethics provided by Allah are in agreement with our moral sense.

## Humans vs animals

Three things distinguish humans from animals:

1. We are **intellectual** beings. We possess the ability to learn, form concepts, and apply logic and reason, which allow us to solve problems, innovate, plan, make decisions, and use language to communicate.

2. We have an **aesthetic** sense. Since time immemorial, we have been producing art. We beautify things, including ourselves. This sense creates music, poetry, artwork, cities, houses, dresses, interiors, etc. It impacts us psychologically.

3. We are **moral** beings. We can differentiate between right and wrong, good and evil. This is the basis for all types of relationships: with Allah, family, friends, neighbors, society, and the world.

## Who sets the standard for right and wrong?

- Fundamental morality is given by Allah when He created us. This is a common asset among humanity. That's the only way we can define moral behavior; otherwise, it will be all relative, and we cannot find a common ground.

وَنَفْسٍ وَمَا سَوَّاهَا ۞ فَأَلْهَمَهَا فُجُورَهَا وَتَقْوَاهَا

And by the soul, when We fashioned it, We inspired it with its evil and its good (Quran 91:7-8)

إِنَّا هَدَيْنَاهُ السَّبِيلَ إِمَّا شَاكِرًا وَإِمَّا كَفُورًا

Indeed, We showed him the way of good and evil, now its up to him to be either grateful or disbelieve (Quran 76:3)

- When Allah created the first human being, He bestowed this faculty on us at the time of our creation.
- Just as we enjoy and appreciate different forms of art, beautify our houses, and learn languages, we can tell evil from good.
- We love, respect, and admire, and appreciate what is good.
- We create justice systems to curb evil in society.
- Fundamental morality is innate and universal, but its implementation in society can take different forms.

## Example of applying the basic morals

- Being good to parents is a fundamental moral value or ethic we all agree on. However, it manifests in different ways across societies.
- In Asia, it may mean keeping them with you at home, and in North America, it may mean visiting them and doing their grocery shopping.

Being kind to others is a basic moral value. Research how kindness is displayed differently across cultures and collect a few examples. You can also take another example instead of kindness.

## Allah gives details through Messengers and Books

إِنَّ هَذَا الْقُرْآنَ يَهْدِي لِلَّتِي هِيَ أَقْوَمُ وَيُبَشِّرُ الْمُؤْمِنِينَ الَّذِينَ يَعْمَلُونَ الصَّالِحَاتِ أَنَّ لَهُمْ أَجْرًا كَبِيرًا

Undoubtedly, this Quran guides to the most upright path and gives glad tidings of a great reward to those among its believers who do good deeds. (Quran 17:9)

- Human beings have a natural tendency to differ in how they interpret this innate moral sense and apply it in their societies across different periods.
- On top of this God-gifted sense, Allah explained good and evil through His Messengers and Book.
- This guidance is now eternally saved in the Quran and is entirely compatible with our inner moral compass.
- There is a consensus among humans on these morals/ethics.
- Differences among societies arise from a preference for one value over another. That does not negate the value's presence. For example, in one society, human freedom may be preferred over modesty. That does not mean that people do not want to be modest as a society.

## Example of Abel and Cain

- The two sons of Adam, Abel (Habeel) and Cain (Qabeel), argued over who would present the sacrifice to their Lord.
- Allah accepted Abel's sacrifice due to his piety.
- Cain got angry about this and killed Abel out of jealousy.

- Abel did not resist even in self-defense, as he knew that hitting or killing someone is morally wrong (though not a good example).
- Cain killed Abel, but soon after, he regretted it.
- He did not want anyone to see this, so he was worried about how to hide the dead body of his brother.
- A crow bird, while digging the earth, showed him how to bury his brother's dead body.
- What we learn from this story is that people often invent excuses to commit evil against their nature, but deep down, they realize they have done something wrong.

## A parable from the Hadith

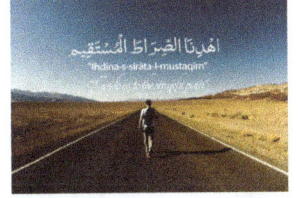

Prophet Muhammad described a parable about staying on the straight path, which is the path of goodness and avoiding evil: "A straight path is something that leads to the destination a person wants to reach. On both sides are high walls with doors, on which curtains are hung. At the end of the path, a caller is calling out to walk straight. If a person wants to lift one of the curtains, a caller from the top says: "Beware! Do not lift the curtains. If you lift them, you will go inside."

The explanation is:
- The straight path is Islam.
  - The walls are the limits Allah prescribes, and the doors are His prohibitions.
  - The caller from the top is the counselor of Allah, who is found in the heart of every human being.
  - And the caller at the end of the path is the Quran.

- That's why we make this supplication (O Allah, guide us to the straight path) at least 17 times a day in our Salah to avoid following other paths.
- The Quran provides ethical/moral guidelines that people can adopt in accordance with their own cultures and practices. The guidelines are universal and fully compatible with human nature. The Quran trusts the human intellect to implement these principles in their lives.

# Our relationship with Allah

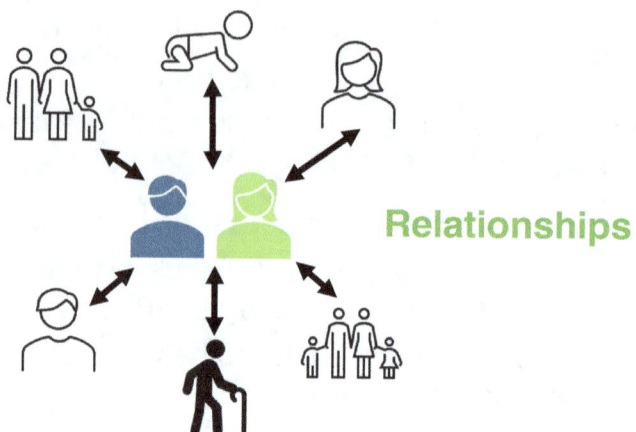

**Relationships**

- The concept of morality is deeply tied to the relationships that we have around us: family, relatives, neighbors, friends, colleagues, fellow citizens, tribesmen, people from other countries, animals, the environment, etc.
- These relationships test our moral behavior.
- The excellence in our moral behavior is directly linked to the closeness of the relationships.
- For example, people who deserve our best conduct are our parents, spouses, children, siblings, cousins, neighbors, and so on.

- Like these relationships, we have **another relationship** that supersedes (takes over) all others, and that is our relationship with Allah.
- He is our Creator, Nurturer, and Owner who gave us everything we have, including our parents.
- It is with this moral sense that we should worship Allah.
- Just as we love our parents because they take care of us and love us, it is our moral obligation to love Allah and dedicate some of our time and life to Him.
- So, for a Muslim, the complete picture of their life is:

 **+ Allah**

## Allah's attributes and human beings

- We cannot comprehend (understand) Allah's being, but we can comprehend His attributes to some extent because we possess these attributes to some extent.
- Allah is all good, and it is an honor for human beings that they also possess some of those qualities that Allah chose for Himself.
- People who purify their souls and continue to build their moral character become closer to Allah because of these attributes.
- When we practice these attributes, we manifest our true nature, which Allah has created us.
- Evil/Wrong that humans commit is nothing but the lack of these attributes in us.

| **Peaceful** | **Generous** | **Merciful** |
|---|---|---|
| **Embracing** | **Just** | **Righteous** |
| **Patient** | **Kind** | **Loving** |
| **Grateful** | **Helper** | **Forgiving** |

# Building character is a lifelong struggle

- Acquiring good traits for building character and keeping them is a lifelong struggle.
- We face different situations every day that test our morals.
- Strengthening character is a two-step process:
  - Get rid of bad habits and negative traits.
  - Develop and nourish good habits and positive traits.
- Keep in mind that no bad deed is SMALL & no good deed is SMALL.
- Also, when doing good, remove this concept: "I am doing it for Allah"; you are actually doing it for yourself, as it will benefit you in this world and the Hereafter.
- Do it "for the sake of Allah".
- Get help with prayers and patience, as this is the recipe given in the Quran to people who face challenges.

  (To remain on the straight path) seek assistance from patience and prayers. (2:45)

  وَ اسْتَعِيْنُوْا بِالصَّبْرِ وَ الصَّلٰوةِ

- A strong faith in Allah plays a critical role in building strong character.
- Our faith and character are tested throughout our lives. Strong faith in Allah builds a strong character that can weather powerful storms, meaning difficult situations.

## Quick Recap

- We are born with the innate (built-in) capability to differentiate between right and wrong, good and evil – we are moral beings.
- Through His prophets and books, Allah gave us the fundamentals of Islamic ethics that we can use to judge our actions against.
- Ethics and morals are compatible with human nature and are universal phenomena. Differences arise from the implementation of a principle across cultures and societies.
- Morality is primarily related to our relationship with Allah and with humans in a different capacity: we respect our mother because we love her, and we worship Allah because we love Him.
- Allah is All-Good, and He bestowed many good qualities in us from the qualities He chose for Himself.
- Building character is a lifelong journey, and we should seek assistance from Allah.

# Chapter 3

# Islamic Etiquette

This chapter covers Islamic etiquette and how religious and cultural etiquette differ.

# Religious and Cultural Etiquette (Customs)

- Religious customs should not be confused with local/cultural customs. They are separate.

## Local/Cultural Customs

- Various displays of regular, patterned behavior, conduct, and manners within a group are called customs and traditions.
- Every human civilization has customs and traditions, without exception.
- Every culture is distinguished from others by its customs.
- Most customs have long histories, and people do not even know when they began.
- When religious people adopt a local culture, they often lose the distinction and try to associate it with religion, which is not right.

## Religious Customs

- The religion revealed to the prophets of Allah directed their respective believers to follow certain customs and etiquette as part of religious guidance and identity.
- The purpose is to remember Allah, purify the soul through worship, mutual love, and respect.
- These customs have been transmitted to us through the consensus and constant practice of the Prophet's companions and the generations that followed.
- Sometimes, when religion becomes part of culture, people often take it as a cultural custom, but it will always remain religious in nature.

## Examples of religious customs

- Declaring the name of Allah before eating and drinking, and praising and thanking Him after eating/drinking.
- Saying Assalam O Alaikum when we meet.
- Saying specific expressions when sneezing and their response.
- Various hygiene-related practices, such as making Wudu before Salah.
- Following specific instructions for cleaning when using the bathroom.
- Following specific instructions to bury the dead.
- Two Eid Festivals.
- Besides Islam, other belief systems, such as Christianity and Hinduism, also have their own religious customs.

## Examples of cultural customs

- Kissing your parents' hands or forehead when seeing them (Arabs).
- Sharing a meal of Turkey with your family and friends on Thanksgiving (US).
- Women are not allowed to leave their houses without permission (Eastern).
- Bowing to each other when meeting (Japan).
- Running of the bulls on the streets of Pamplona, Spain (Spain).
- Kite flying competition on Basant (Punjab, India, and Pakistan).
- Slurping the noodles to enjoy them (China)
- Show up 15-20 minutes late to the party, or be called greedy (Venezuela).

Pick a country or nation and write about one or more of its interesting cultural customs.

# Islamic Etiquette (Customs)

- In this section, we will cover some Islamic customs and explain the difference between their religious and cultural aspects.

## Eating Etiquette - Religious Customs

بِسْمِ ٱللَّه
(I begin) with the name of Allah

الحمدُ لِلَّهِ
All thanks belong to Allah

- Saying '*Bismillah*' before eating or drinking anything – Muslims remember Allah all the time, especially when a blessing is given, and food is the best blessing one can have.
- Eat with your RIGHT hand – Muslims are reminded that on the day of Judgment, people who received good grades will be given their results in their right hand.
- Even if you are left-handed, try to develop the habit of eating with your right hand.
- Thanking Allah (*AlhamduLillah*) after finishing a meal or drink reminds Muslims that it's only Allah who has bestowed countless blessings on us, and that it is our moral obligation to thank Him.
- The guidance is given through the Sunnah.
- Most Muslims across the world practice it regardless of culture and geography. Religious customs are usually universal.

## Other Eating Manners – Some Cultural Customs

- If you are sharing a meal on a large plate, eat only from your side (as many cultures do).
- Allow older people to take the food first.
- Avoid distractions such as using your phone or watching TV, and enjoy Allah's blessing.
- Serve younger siblings if you are old enough.
- Don't make noises while chewing.
- Take only enough of what you can eat and finish.

## Salutation and Greeting Among Muslims - Religious

وعليكم السلام رحمة الله    السلام عليكم ورحمة الله
Peace, Mercy and Blessings of Allah upon you
وبركاته

- When Muslims meet each other (men, women), they say a prayer of peace and well-being for one another in this world and the Hereafter by saying:
- Assalam O Alaikum Wa Rehmatullah Wa Barakatahu. → One who initiates
- Wa Alaikum Assalam Wa Rehmatullah Wa Barakatahu → Reply
- Saying the first part is necessary, the rest is recommended.
- The guidance of this greeting is given through Sunnah and also mentioned in the Quran.

## Other Salutation and Greeting Manners - Cultural

- Young people should say Salam to elders; people walking should say Salam to those sitting.
- Someone smaller should say Salam to a larger group.
- Say Salam as much as possible.
- Say Salam to everyone, whether you know them or not.
- Shaking hands and hugging are optional and go with the local culture.
- This is the oldest practice since the time of Prophet Adam.

## Utterance after Sneezing - Religious Customs

All thanks are due to Allah.

May Allah have mercy on you.

May Allah guide you and keep your affairs well (Optional).

- Sneezing relieves a person from an internal disorder.
- The person who sneezes says "**Alhamdulillah**," and the person who hears them says "**Yarhamukallah**."
- Since an internal disorder has been restored, we are asked to praise Allah SWT and be grateful to Him for this restoration.
- The person hearing this is praying for the person sneezing.
- The guidance is given through the Sunnah and is among the oldest traditions since the time of Adam.
- It is said that when Allah blew His soul into Adam, and He opened up his eyes in this world, he sneezed and said Alhamdulillah.

## Other manners of sneezing - Cultural Customs

- Cover your mouth when sneezing.
- Say Alhamdulillah a little louder so other people can make dua for you while hearing it.
- Saying AlhamduLillah and responding once is enough.
- Trying to minimize the sound of sneezing.
- You can still follow other cultural practices besides saying AlhamduLillah. E.g., saying 'Excuse me' when sneezing in public.

## Instructions on personal hygiene

- Allah SWT wants us to be physically purified, also. The following instructions are part of the custom now:

    - Clipping the mustache.
    - Trimming or maintaining your beard (if you keep it).
    - Removing the pubic hair (when you hit puberty).
    - Removing hair under the arm (armpit).
    - Clipping the fingernails and toenails.
    - Circumcising male offspring.
    - Keep our teeth clean.
    - Keep our nostrils and mouth clean.
    - Cleaning ourselves after using the bathroom. (Using water is the most hygienic way of doing it.)

الطُّهُورُ شَطْرُ الإِيمَانِ

Purity is half of faith. (Hadith, Sahih Muslim 223)

- If there is one word that represents the religion of Islam, that would be 'purification' or 'cleanliness'.
- Islam is the religion of human nature, and human beings tend to be clean and are usually sensitive about it.
- We are asked to follow these hygiene instructions as much as possible, depending on the situation.
- That's why some of these instructions are included as part of Ablution (Wudu).
- The best method should be used to keep your teeth clean (there is a misconception about miswak).
- Some of these hygiene instructions have a direct impact on our "moral looks" also (beard & mustache).

Indeed, Allah loves those who turn in repentance and those who purify themselves. (Quran 2:222)

إِنَّ اللَّهَ يُحِبُّ التَّوَّابِينَ وَيُحِبُّ الْمُتَطَهِّرِينَ

## Other customs

- Taking a bath after the menstrual cycle is over (girls only).
- Taking a bath after seminal discharge (boys only).
- Bathing the dead body before burial.
- Enshrouding the dead body in a coffin cloth before burial.
- Praying on the dead body before burial.
- Burying the dead.

## Celebrating Festivals

- Prophet Muhammad originated these two festivals as instructed by God.
- Previous Muslim nations (Jews and Christians) also had their festivals on various occasions.
- The two festivals celebrate the two greatest acts of obedience and piety.

## Eid Al-Fitr

- Eid al-Fitr is celebrated after Ramadan.
- One must pay Zakat al-Fitr before the Eid prayer on behalf of every member of the immediate family.
- People should start saying *Takbiraat* before the Eid prayer.
- The Imam would lead two units of Eid prayers and deliver sermons afterward.
- People wear new clothes, decorate houses, prepare special food, and share the blessings of Allah with others.

## Eid Al-Adha

- It commemorates the sacrifice Ibrahim (AS) made when he wanted to slaughter his son, Ismail, for the sake of Allah.
- It coincides with the great event of Hajj.
- People offer animal sacrifice (hence it is called Eid Al-Adha).
- People should start saying special *Takbiraat* during the days of *Tashreeq* (3 days after the Eid prayers).
- People wear new clothes, decorate houses, prepare special food, and share the blessings of Allah with others.

Why has Allah given instructions about things that are quite personal in nature?

# Chapter 4

# Basic Manners

This chapter covers basic manners that everyone should learn, regardless of race or religion, because following them helps build a better society. We will also learn the Islamic teachings about them.

# The Human Bond

- While religion and race provide identity, the "human bond" is built on the universal experiences we all share.
- People identify with a tribe or a country, but as humans, we are all part of one large family.
- The human bond is an invisible thread of empathy that connects us when we see someone else in pain or celebrating a success, even if they look or believe differently from us.
- We are bonded to different people through different relationships, and Morals are about fulfilling rights according to the nature of each relationship.

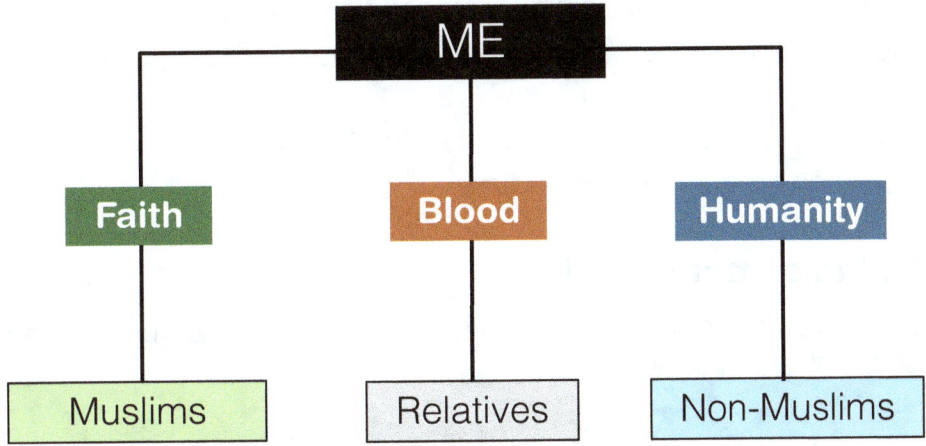

- One relationship is often misunderstood, and that is our relationship with non-Muslims. We have an unbroken bond with all of humanity: we are all children of Adam, so we are all either siblings or cousins. We must fulfill all the rights of a non-Muslim due to this relationship.
- Some Ahadith of Prophet Muhammad are mistakenly applied to the non-Muslims of our times when it comes to greeting them or having a social bond with them. In those days, due to a special law, Allah prohibited these acts for the disbelievers of Prophet Muhammad.
- Today, if you initiate the greeting, you can say what is prevalent in society. For example, Hello, Hi, Good Morning, All the Best, etc.
- If they initiate the greeting and say Assalam O Alaikum to you, you can respond with Wa Alaikum Assalam (because it's a dua valid for everyone).

How can we strengthen the bond of humanity with people of other faiths?

# Manners and Etiquette

## When visiting someone

- Visiting manners vary according to your relationship with the host, but common courtesies should prevail.
- Inform them in advance if it's possible.
- It is recommended to bring gifts with you, as they increase love in relationships.
- Pick a time to visit that is convenient for them to host you.
- Always say Salam to everyone when entering the house.
- Introduce yourself if you are visiting for the very first time.
- Stay in the area of the house/place where they want to host you – respect their privacy.
- Thank them for their generosity and make dua for them.
- Always arrive on time and leave on time.

## When visiting someone sick

- When visiting someone sick, additionally, you should make dua for them as taught by Prophet Muhammad.

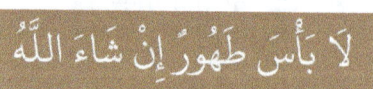

لَا بَأْسَ طَهُورٌ إِنْ شَاءَ اللَّهُ

**Don't worry, it will result in purification, God-willing.**

## When someone visits us

- Guests are considered 'Mercy from God' in Islam.
- Greet them warmly, welcome them into your home, and show them to a comfortable, appropriate room.
- No guest should leave without you serving them the best food and drinks that you have.
- Make them comfortable by asking them in advance if they need anything.
- Prophet Muhammad used to honor guests by offering them a seat.
- Traditionally, hospitality is the virtue that distinguishes Muslims from other nations.

# Guidance from Quran and Prophet's Best Example

يَا أَيُّهَا الَّذِينَ آمَنُوا لَا تَدْخُلُوا بُيُوتًا غَيْرَ بُيُوتِكُمْ حَتَّىٰ تَسْتَأْنِسُوا وَتُسَلِّمُوا عَلَىٰ أَهْلِهَا ۚ ذَٰلِكُمْ خَيْرٌ لَّكُمْ لَعَلَّكُمْ تَذَكَّرُونَ

فَإِن لَّمْ تَجِدُوا فِيهَا أَحَدًا فَلَا تَدْخُلُوهَا حَتَّىٰ يُؤْذَنَ لَكُمْ ۖ وَإِن قِيلَ لَكُمُ ارْجِعُوا فَارْجِعُوا ۖ هُوَ أَزْكَىٰ لَكُمْ

وَاللَّهُ بِمَا تَعْمَلُونَ عَلِيمٌ

O Believers, do not enter other people's houses until you ask permission and say Salam to them. You should remind yourself. But if you don't find anyone or don't get permission, do not enter. And if you are told to return, then return (without feeling bad about it), it is purer for you. God knows what you do. (Quran 24:27-28)

If one of you seeks permission to enter three times and is denied, let him return. (Hadith, Sahih Bukhari 6245)

Whoever believes in Allah and the Last Day, let him honor his guest. (Sahih al-Bukhari 5673, Muslim 3255)

## Etiquettes of Talking to Others

- Islam taught us to deal with people according to their status and relationship with us.
- In Islam, there is no "one size fits all" etiquette for conversing with others – we honor relationships according to their relative rank/position with us.
- Although our conversations should always be respectful, we are told to show particular respect to our elders.
- Respecting elders is one of Islam's hallmarks.
- Face the person and look into their eyes when holding a conversation.
- Let them finish their talk before you start.
- Be respectful even when talking to friends – have a conversation appropriate to your level of closeness.
- Talking gently with younger children will earn you respect.

## Guidance from Prophet's Best Example

"He is not of us who does not show mercy to young children, nor honor the elderly". (Al-Tirmidhi).

## Think before you speak

- The Quran and Sunnah have placed great emphasis on our conversations, our choice of words, and our attitude toward others when talking.

- We are asked "not to take it lightly" when hurting people through our speech/words.

- When holding a conversation with ANYONE, apply the golden rule: Think before you speak.
- Words are like an arrow – they never return once left the bow.
- Speaking ill of others in their absence (backbiting) is a major sin.
- Mostly, Satan sows the seeds of discord and enmity through words.
- Having positive feelings about others will always result in positive talk – look at their brighter side.
- Controlling the tongue is a huge challenge; staying quiet at times can save you from trouble, regret, and sin.
- Avoid argumentation because this is when you lose control over your tongue.
- Getting control of our anger is the first step in avoiding irrational behavior in our talking.
- Ill-speaking of others can destroy the reward for our worship.
- Asking for forgiveness from Allah and the person is the ONLY way to mend things.
- The Quran admires those who swallow their anger and avoid confrontation when provoked.
- Swallowing anger means that we may become angry, but we must control it because that is our test.
- Your attitude in talking may be the direct manifestation of your level of negative ego – there is a bigger problem at hand.

# Guidance from Quran and Prophet's best example

قَدْ أَفْلَحَ الْمُؤْمِنُونَ الَّذِينَ هُمْ فِي صَلَاتِهِمْ خَاشِعُونَ وَالَّذِينَ هُمْ عَنِ اللَّغْوِ مُعْرِضُونَ

Believers who are humble in their prayers and avoid vain talk and matters have attained success. (23:1-3)

إِذْ يَتَلَقَّى الْمُتَلَقِّيَانِ عَنِ الْيَمِينِ وَعَنِ الشِّمَالِ قَعِيدٌ ۝ مَّا يَلْفِظُ مِن قَوْلٍ إِلَّا لَدَيْهِ رَقِيبٌ عَتِيدٌ

They should realize that two takers are sitting on the right and the left, and no word is uttered by anyone except that it is saved by the watchful guardian. (50:17-18)

وَعِبَادُ الرَّحْمَٰنِ الَّذِينَ يَمْشُونَ عَلَى الْأَرْضِ هَوْنًا وَإِذَا خَاطَبَهُمُ الْجَاهِلُونَ قَالُوا سَلَامًا

And the Servants of the Most Merciful are those who walk on the earth with humility, and when ignorant people invoke them, they say "peace". (25:63)

يَا أَيُّهَا الَّذِينَ آمَنُوا لَا يَسْخَرْ قَوْمٌ مِّن قَوْمٍ عَسَىٰ أَن يَكُونُوا خَيْرًا مِّنْهُمْ وَلَا نِسَاءٌ مِّن نِّسَاءٍ عَسَىٰ أَن يَكُنَّ خَيْرًا مِّنْهُنَّ ۖ وَلَا تَلْمِزُوا أَنفُسَكُمْ وَلَا تَنَابَزُوا بِالْأَلْقَابِ

O Believers, your men should not make fun of other men; perhaps they are better than them; your women should not make fun of other women; perhaps they are better than them. Do not defame one another, nor insult them by using nicknames. (49:11)

Every morning, the rest of the body begs the tongue, saying, Fear Allah concerning us, for we are (dependent) upon you. If you are upright, then we will be upright, and if you are corrupt, then we will be corrupt. (Hadith, Tirmidhi)

Whoever believes in Allah and the Last Day should speak a good word or remain silent. (Hadith, Bukhari & Muslim)

Nothing will topple people headlong into the Hellfire more than "the harvests of their tongues." (Hadith, Tirmidhi & Al-Majah)

## Making a queue

- Islam is all about discipline and organization.
- We learn that, in our daily worship and prayers, we make neat rows as part of the discipline.
- We should practice this discipline when we are gathering in other public places, at schools, at theme parks, at festivals, and when waiting for food.
- Skipping the line or jumping is considered rude and infringes on other people's rights, and must be avoided.
- Do NOT play tricks to skip your position.
- When in the queue, give other people their personal space.
- Manage your anger – this is one of those places.

Do not skip the line!

## Ask before you take

- Being inquisitive, we tend to touch or take things from someone else's place without realizing they don't belong to us.
- It's always nice to ask permission before touching/taking something that doesn't belong to us.
- We do that often with our friends, but it's nice to take permission even from them.
- This also applies when you are occupying someone else's space – entering a room, a house, or a personal space.
- Siblings share each other's clothes, shoes, and gadgets … make it a habit with them also.

**Stealing**

**VS**

**Borrowing**

## Taking responsibility of our actions

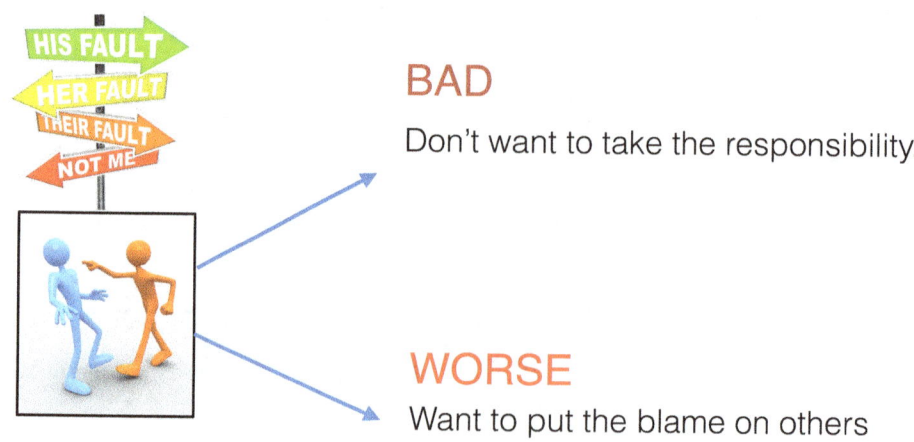

BAD

Don't want to take the responsibility.

WORSE

Want to put the blame on others

- Blaming others for our actions is an easy way out and is considered a short-term 'success'.
- It is usually a consequence of "someone intensely shamed or punished for admitting responsibility for a bad action or a mistake".
- People who blame others usually lack honesty and truthfulness – a bigger problem.
- We should realize that we are all human beings and make mistakes – admitting our mistakes and taking responsibility for our actions is the most natural way to handle them.
- Make this deal with your parents – make honesty 'easy' for me, and I will start taking responsibility for my actions.
- Making mistakes is not a sin, but blaming others and lying are.
- Blaming others when you know they are innocent and letting them face the consequences may become a greater sin.

## Sharing and Caring

- Sharing and caring can be expressed within our social circle or through acts of charity.

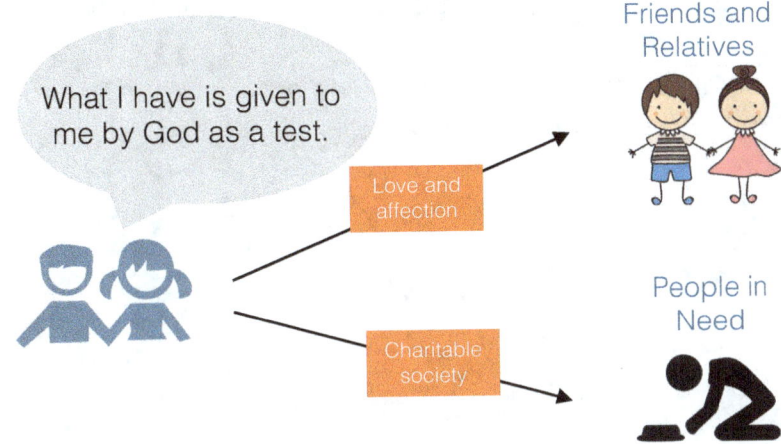

- In virtuous deeds, sharing is at the top of the list.
- The Islamic perspective on wealth and possessions encourages you to share: all my possessions are granted to me by God, and it's a test of how I use them.
- Sharing is not only about money – we can also share our time and our knowledge.
- Sharing softens a person's heart and helps them become a better human being – the effect is larger than just giving.
- Allah bestows blessings on that "thing" shared with others – the results are enormous.
- Mistakenly, 'charity' is often restricted to "giving money to poor people" – whatever you share with your family, friends, neighbors, and colleagues is all considered a charity from you.

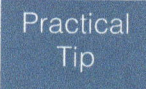

## Guidance from the Prophet's Best Example

Exchange gifts, as that will increase your love for one another. (Hadith Al-Bukhari)

"He is not a believer who eats his fill whilst his neighbor beside him goes hungry." (Hadith Al-Bukhari, #112)

"O Abu Dharr, when you cook a stew, put more water in the broth and take care of your neighbors." (Hadith Sahih Muslim, 2625)

## Netiquettes

- There is a common misconception that saying/doing something bad on social media is not as bad as doing so in person.
- In reality, it has the same effect, and it is much easier to hurt people online than in person.
- Beware! Your social media posts and activities are recorded in two places: One with the company and another with the angels.

**Social Media**
**A blessing**,
**A curse** OR
**A Tool**

"Don't use social media to impress people; use it to impact people."
DaveWillis.org

**Forward**

Share
Use these buttons very carefully

- Islamic ethics and morals are equally applicable to social media; never underestimate its power.
- It is much easier to break the rules online than physically – Satan's job is much easier with social media because sins/rewards multiply faster.
- Use it to stay in touch with your friends and relatives, to discuss and share good and sad moments (within a close circle), and to be a positive force that makes an impact.
- The most common casualty of social media is "modesty" - Satan's first attack is always going to be "remove shame from you".
- The other dangers you could easily fall into when using social media include spreading lies without verifying them, shaming others, creating discord among people, causing scandals, and breaching privacy.

# Guidance from Quran and Prophet's Best Example

يَا أَيُّهَا الَّذِينَ آمَنُوا اجْتَنِبُوا كَثِيرًا مِّنَ الظَّنِّ إِنَّ بَعْضَ الظَّنِّ إِثْمٌ ۖ وَلَا تَجَسَّسُوا وَلَا يَغْتَب بَّعْضُكُم بَعْضًا ۚ أَيُحِبُّ أَحَدُكُمْ أَن يَأْكُلَ لَحْمَ أَخِيهِ مَيْتًا فَكَرِهْتُمُوهُ ۚ

O Believers, avoid suspicion as much as possible because some suspicions are sins. Do not spy (breach privacy) or backbite each other. Would any of you like to eat the flesh of his brother, then despise it? (49:12)

وَلَا تَقْفُ مَا لَيْسَ لَكَ بِهِ عِلْمٌ ۚ إِنَّ السَّمْعَ وَالْبَصَرَ وَالْفُؤَادَ كُلُّ أُولَٰئِكَ كَانَ عَنْهُ مَسْئُولًا

Don't pursue anything that you do not have any knowledge of because you will be asked about your hearing, seeing, and thinking (then how about speaking). (17:36)

A person does not cover another person's faults in the world, but Allah will cover his faults on the Day of Judgment." (Hadith Al-Muslim, #2590)

The Messenger of Allah asked his companions: "Do you know what is backbiting?"
They said, "Allah and His Messenger know best."
He said, "Mentioning your brother, what he would hate."
One of the companions asked, "What if what I say about my brother is true?"
He replied, "If what you say is true, you have backbit him, and if it is not true, you have slandered him." (Hadith Sahi Muslim #2589)

## Let our manners speak for us

- Our manners determine the kind of relationships we have with the people around us.
- Our manners shape our personality.
- Our actions/dealings directly reflect how good/bad a person we are on the inside.

- Manners are part of the first impression we get of someone we meet.
- Self-assessment and looking at our own faults always help us see other people's goodness.
- We are not "educated" if we don't have manners.
- Silence is powerful; it speaks volumes. Be a good listener.
- Your mood should not be reflected in your manners.

## Quick Recap

- Morals are about fulfilling rights in accordance with the nature of the relationship.
- We have many bonds with people around us: blood, faith, and humanity.
- Guests are considered 'Mercy from God' in Islam.
- Taking a gift (e.g., food to share) when visiting someone can increase love and affection.
- Respecting our elders is one of the hallmarks of Islam.
- Controlling your tongue is a huge challenge; staying quiet at times can save you from trouble, regret, and sin.
- Blaming others for our actions is an easy way out and is considered a short-term 'success,' but it ultimately shapes our personality.
- Allah SWT puts blessings in that "thing" that is shared with others.
- Islamic ethics and morals are equally applicable to social media – never underestimate it.

Everything has positives and negatives. Write down the advantages and disadvantages of Social Media and suggest a few things on how we can benefit from it.

# Chapter 5

# Humility and Humbleness

This chapter covers one of the most fundamental traits that Allah wants in us, and that is the foundation of our relationship with Allah.

# Humility and humbleness

## The concept

- Humility and humbleness (being humble) are used interchangeably, but humility is an inner feeling that resides in our hearts and is expressed in humbleness.

- CS Lewis beautifully said, "Humility is not thinking less of yourself but thinking of yourself less."
- The opposite is arrogance and being proud.
- Total submission to Allah requires humility, or in other words, only humility allows a person to achieve complete submission to Allah.
- People who think they are better than others lack humility.
- Humility does not mean low self-esteem.

## Humility is the hallmark of a believer

وَعِبَادُ الرَّحْمَٰنِ الَّذِينَ يَمْشُونَ عَلَى الْأَرْضِ هَوْنًا وَإِذَا خَاطَبَهُمُ الْجَاهِلُونَ قَالُوا سَلَامًا

And the servants of the Most Merciful are those who walk on the earth with humility, and when ignorant people try to provoke them, they separate themselves by saying, "peace". (Quran 25:63)

إِنَّمَا يَخْشَى اللَّهَ مِنْ عِبَادِهِ الْعُلَمَاءُ

The reality is that only those among the servants of Allah will fear Allah (show humility) who possess true knowledge (about Allah). (Quran 35:28)

- Allah's true servants walk on the earth with humility.
- Believers in leadership positions should demonstrate humility above all.
- Pondering over Allah's creation results in humility.
- Knowledge of Allah, His creation, and ourselves makes us humble.
- Humility comes from comprehending the awe, grandeur, and majesty of Allah.
- It also comes from knowing about oneself and one's faults and weaknesses.
- Realizing that Allah is in full control of everything, including ourselves, keeps our attitude in check and makes us humble.

## Believer = Humble Person

Humility is at the center of many virtues

**Gratitude**
With all my weaknesses, Allah has granted me so many blessings without even asking for them.

**Piety**
As a human being, I am weak. Will I be able to face Allah on the day of Judgment?

**HUMILITY**

**Forgiveness**
With all His power and might, if Allah forgives people all the time, then who am I?

**Trust in Allah**
It's only Allah who is in full control, not me, so I should hand over my matters to Him after making sincere efforts.

## Worship and Humility

- If we truly know who Allah is, then we can never be arrogant.
- Allah asked us to be humble at all times.
- It is humility in our hearts before Allah that encourages us to worship Him.
- All worship rituals are just the symbolic expressions of that humility before Allah.

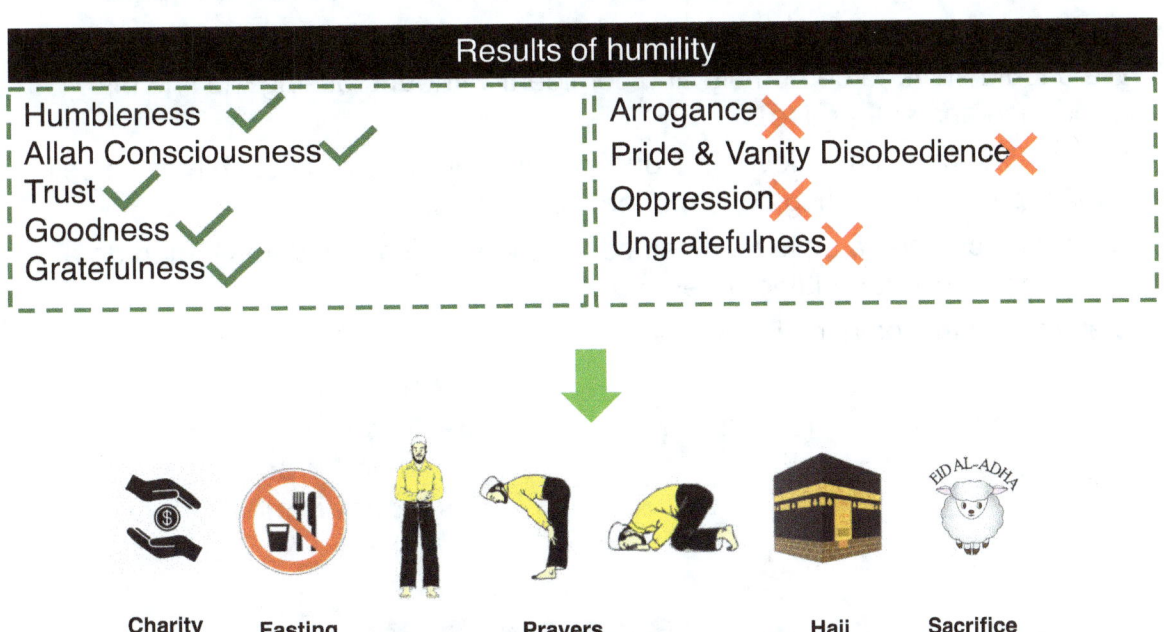

**Results of humility**

Humbleness ✓
Allah Consciousness ✓
Trust ✓
Goodness ✓
Gratefulness ✓

Arrogance ✗
Pride & Vanity Disobedience ✗
Oppression ✗
Ungratefulness ✗

Charity    Fasting    Prayers    Hajj    Sacrifice

- In the Quran, Allah told us why He created us:

وَ مَا خَلَقْتُ الْجِنَّ وَ الْاِنْسَ اِلَّا لِيَعْبُدُونِ

I have created the jinn and men **only** to worship Me (51:56)

- In Arabic, worship is called 'Ibadah.' Its form, 'Ubudiyyah,' means to express one's humility or humbleness as a slave. A complete sense of humility overcomes a person who completely submits to the will of Allah. When Allah says He wants us to worship Him, it means living a humble life and never showing arrogance. It does not mean that we are asked to pray all the time.

Do you remember why Shaytan refused to obey Allah and not bow down to Adam, and what reasons did he give?

## Humility and self-esteem

- Self-confidence and self-esteem are as important as humility, but we should know the difference.
- Humility does not mean weakness; it simply shows the lack of false pride.
- Arrogance is "rejecting the truth and despising people."
- We should strive to be humble and confident without crossing the line into arrogance and self-praise.
- When Allah raises a believer in worldly status, humility protects him from self-praise, pride, and feelings of superiority over others.
- Humility increases a believer's self-confidence, which motivates him to do all that is good without putting others down.
- Maintaining this balance is the trial.

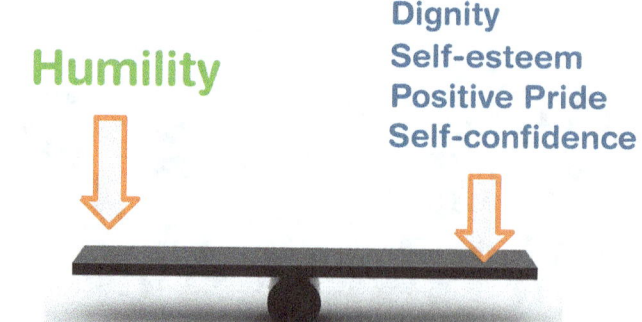

**Balance** **all these positive traits with** humility.

# Guidance from Quran and the Prophet's Example

قَدْ أَفْلَحَ الْمُؤْمِنُونَ الَّذِينَ هُمْ فِي صَلَاتِهِمْ خَاشِعُونَ

Successful indeed are the believers who humble themselves in their prayers. (Quran 23:1-2)

فَإِلَهُكُمْ إِلَهٌ وَاحِدٌ فَلَهُ أَسْلِمُواْ وَبَشِّرِ الْمُخْبِتِينَ

So remember, your Lord is one Lord, so submit to Him and give glad tidings to those who humble themselves. (Quran 22:34)

Shall I not tell you about the companions of Paradise? They will be humble persons considered weak, but if they give an oath by Allah, it will be fulfilled. Shall I not tell you about the companions of Hellfire? They are harsh, haughty, and arrogant people. (Hadith: Sahih Bukhari 4634)

Verily, Allah has revealed that you must be humble towards one another so that no one wrongs another or boasts to another. (Hadith: Sahih Muslim 2865)

The Prophet lived a very simple and humble life in Makkah as a trader before his Prophethood and in Medinah as the Head of the State after being commissioned as Allah's Messenger. The change in his social status from that of a trader in Makkah to the Head of the State in Medinah did not bring any change in his humble living. Umar reported that once the Prophet said, "Do not admire me as did the Christians admire Jesus, the son of Mary; I am only a slave, so say 'the Slave of Allah and His Messenger.'" (Seerah of Prophet Muhammad)

Before accepting Islam, when *Adiyy ibn Haatim*, the leader of a tribe, came to see the Prophet, he called him inside his house. A maidservant brought a cushion for the Prophet to rest on, but the Prophet placed it between him and Adiyy and sat on the floor. Adiyy later said that he immediately realized that the Prophet did not behave like a king. (Seerah of Prophet Muhammad)

# From the life of companions of the Prophet

Umar (RA) was marching upon Damascus with his army. Abu Ubaydah ibn Al-Jarrah (RA) was with him. They came upon a little lake. Umar descended from his camel, removed his shoes, tied them together, and hung them on his shoulder. He took the reins of his camel, and together they entered the water. Seeing this happening before the army, Abu Ubaydah said, "O commander of the faithful, how can you be so humble in front of all your men?" Umar answered, "Woe, Abu Ubaydah, if anyone else thinks this way! Thoughts like this will cause the downfall of the Muslims. Don't you see? We were indeed a very lowly people. Allah raised us to honor and greatness through Islam. If we forget who we are and wish other than Islam, which elevated us, the One who raised us surely will debase us.

When Umar's army freed the people of Jerusalem, they asked Umar to collect the keys to the city. Umar proceeded alone to Jerusalem with one slave, and between them they had only one camel, which they rode turn by turn. As they approached the city where the Muslim Commanders were to meet Umar, it was the turn of the slave to ride. The slave wanted Umar to ride the camel, but Umar refused. As they came to the city, the people saw the strange display of humility: the slave rode the camel while the Caliph walked, holding the camel's rope.

## Quick Recap

- Humility is an inner feeling that resides in our hearts and is expressed in humility.
- Total submission to Allah requires humility, or in other words, only humility allows one to achieve complete submission.
- Humility is at the center of many virtues: gratitude, patience, forgiveness, trust, etc.
- Knowledge of Allah, His creation, and ourselves makes us humble.
- All forms of worship are just symbolic expressions of "worship," which comes from humility in front of Allah.
- Self-confidence and self-esteem are as important as humility, but we should know the difference.
- Knowing the definitions and concepts of arrogance and vanity helps us avoid falling into them.
- All such positive traits, such as self-confidence, dignity, self-esteem, and pride, MUST be balanced by Humility.
- We should study the lives of our Prophet and his companions to understand that, despite ruling over the entire civilized world at that time, they were all very humble people.

You just won a competition after putting a lot of effort into it. This is a proud moment. What steps can you take to remain humble during this time?

# Chapter 6

# Gratitude / Shukr

This chapter covers the concept of gratitude, or shukr, and why it is a test from Allah for everyone, especially for those who are blessed.

# The concept of Gratitude - (*Shukr*) شكر

## General definition

Gratitude is recognizing the value of things or positive life experiences we did not ask for or work towards, yet we still receive.

- Gratitude is not only the greatest of all virtues but the mother of all virtues.
- The foundation of our relationship with Allah and with the people around us must be based on gratitude.
- Love is the natural result of the feeling of gratitude in our hearts. It is said that "love is a light in a heart filled with gratitude."
- It is also termed as "being thankful" or "being grateful."

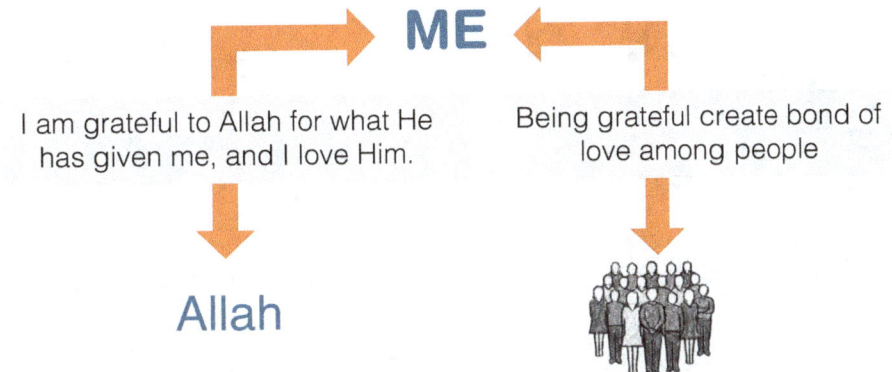

**ME**

I am grateful to Allah for what He has given me, and I love Him.

Being grateful create bond of love among people

Allah

## Being grateful to Allah is an attitude

- Like humility, gratitude is one of the fundamentals on which our relationship with Allah is founded – it results in our prayers and other forms of worship, which we do out of love for Him. Without humility, we can never be grateful.
- This gratitude and love are expressed through our hearts, our tongues, and our actions.
- It is not possible that we love Allah for what He has given us, and we utter the words of gratitude with our tongue, but our actions are not compatible with these feelings.
- We usually focus on what is missing; we should carefully remind ourselves of the blessings we already have.
- The Quran has strongly emphasized this virtue for a believing Muslim.
- One way to express our gratitude through our actions is to not misuse the blessings of Allah – for example, if tongue and speech are blessings, they should not be misused.

## AlhamduLillah – all the time

- In Islam, we do not associate our gratitude towards Allah just with 'favorable things' or 'positive life experiences' – It is required in all conditions.
- With our limited knowledge, we don't know what is 'favorable' or 'positive' for us.

وَمَا بِكُم مِّن نِّعْمَةٍ فَمِنَ اللَّهِ

"and whatever you have of favor - it is from Allah." (An-Nahl: 53)

**The Gratitude is for Allah Alone**

## The Greatest Blessing(s)

Prophet
# Muhammad

- ISLAM is the greatest blessing of Allah upon humanity.
- Islam brings humanity from the darkness of ignorance to the light of faith.
- This blessing alone should be enough to love Allah, as through Islam, we come to know Him and know the actions that we can do to earn His paradise.

- Prophet Muhammad is the one who gave us Islam and the Quran.
- He went through oppression, suffering, and wars so Islam could reach us through generations.
- The best way we can show our gratitude to him is to love him and follow his instructions.

- If you think about it, there is a lot to be thankful for. We have more than what we lack. Allah repeated this statement multiple times in the form of a question – a method usually meant to emphasize something that was already obvious, but we were missing the point.

So (O humans and jinns), which of the splendors of your Lord will you deny? (Quran 55:13)

فَبِأَيِّ آلَاءِ رَبِّكُمَا تُكَذِّبَانِ

What is the greatest blessing in your life?

# Be grateful in your life

## Gratitude of heart, tongue, and actions

### Hear

- It all starts here.
- Live in the present moment and learn to enjoy the little things that we may lose one day.
- Love your Creator.
- Should encourage us and help us in our prayers.

### Speech

- Saying "AlhamduLillah" every time we enjoy a blessing with a full understanding of the blessings that we have.
- Say a kind word.
- Remember Allah through duas.
- Do not complain all the time.

### Action

- Share your blessings with others. Help others with money, time, and love.
- Give someone a gift in return for a favor they did for you.
- Do not use blessings in disobeying Allah.
- Don't be extravagant.

## Gratitude is a trial from Allah

- Islam takes gratitude to the next level because our attitude towards the blessings of Allah has severe consequences in the Hereafter.
- Allah has made this world a trial for us.
- Sorrow and happiness, poverty and riches, grief, and joy, which continuously befall people in this world, are all tests from Allah.
- When He blesses someone with affluence and status, He tests whether such people will remain grateful to Him or not.
- If they end up proud and arrogant, misuse their blessings, and do not use them for the benefit of others, then they will miserably fail in this test on the day of judgment.
- If we align our perspective on this life with this practice of Allah and remain mindful, it will help us live happily and achieve success in the hereafter.
- The best attitude is not to take any blessing for granted.

> Be grateful because it's a test from Allah, and He is watching your attitude.

**ISLAM**

> Be grateful because it is a good thing to do, and you live happily.

## Gratitude to fellow human beings

- As human beings, we have unwritten contracts of rights and responsibilities with other human beings, but many people in our lives go beyond this contract.
- Some of those people are: our parents, siblings, teachers, mentors, Imams and scholars, close friends, uncles/aunts and cousins, and people who indirectly influence our lives (cotton growers, farmers, medical doctors, etc.).
- Our focus should not be on a few people who have done something bad to us, but on many others from whom we take benefits day in and day out.
- Being grateful to others creates a bond of love that is otherwise missing from the relationship.
- The "thanks" should not only be restricted to Muslims and relatives.

## Gratitude to our parents

- In Islam, we are asked to be kind to our parents, and we cannot be kind to them if we are not grateful to them first.
- In the Quran, when Allah talks about His directives for us, parents are often mentioned immediately after Allah.
- For all they do for us, it is this deep feeling of gratitude that creates the unbroken bond of love with our parents.
- This feeling of gratitude and love cannot be confined to our hearts and our tongues; it must be expressed through our actions.

## Guidance from the Quran

وَوَصَّيْنَا الْإِنسَانَ بِوَالِدَيْهِ حَمَلَتْهُ أُمُّهُ وَهْنًا عَلَىٰ وَهْنٍ وَفِصَالُهُ فِي عَامَيْنِ أَنِ اشْكُرْ لِي وَلِوَالِدَيْكَ إِلَيَّ

Indeed, we have counseled human beings about their parents. His/her mother carried him/her with pain and difficulty and then suckled him/her for two years. So, be grateful to your parents and me, and remember you will be returned to Me. (18:7)

وَقَضَىٰ رَبُّكَ أَلَّا تَعْبُدُوا إِلَّا إِيَّاهُ وَبِالْوَالِدَيْنِ إِحْسَانًا ۚ إِمَّا يَبْلُغَنَّ عِندَكَ الْكِبَرَ أَحَدُهُمَا أَوْ كِلَاهُمَا فَلَا تَقُل لَّهُمَا أُفٍّ وَلَا تَنْهَرْهُمَا وَقُل لَّهُمَا قَوْلًا كَرِيمًا وَاخْفِضْ لَهُمَا جَنَاحَ الذُّلِّ مِنَ الرَّحْمَةِ وَقُل رَّبِّ ارْحَمْهُمَا كَمَا رَبَّيَانِي صَغِيرًا

And [remember that] your Lord has enjoined you to worship none but Him, and to treat well your parents. If either or both of them attain old age in your life before you, show them no sign of impatience, nor scold them while answering; but speak to them with good etiquette and lower your wings of humility from mercy for them and say: "Lord, be merciful to them the way they nursed me in childhood. " (17:23-24)

## Blessings – count them if you can

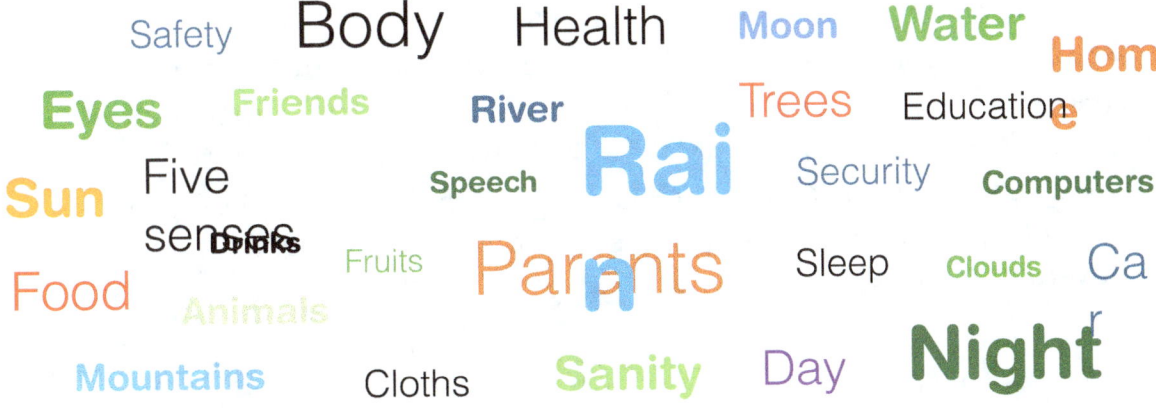

- We must look deep and wide and find the blessings that we should be grateful for.

وَآتَاكُم مِّن كُلِّ مَا سَأَلْتُمُوهُ ۚ وَإِن تَعُدُّوا نِعْمَتَ اللَّهِ لَا تُحْصُوهَا ۗ إِنَّ الْإِنسَانَ لَظَلُومٌ كَفَّارٌ

And He gave you all you asked of Him. And if you were to count the blessings of Allah, you could not enumerate them. Indeed, mankind is most unjust and ungrateful. (Quran 14:34)

## Beware of your blessings

- We tend to consider material blessings as the only blessings.
- MONEY AND MATERIAL THINGS ARE NOT THE <u>ONLY</u> BLESSINGS.
- We tend to forget many blessings until we lose them.
- When we get sick, we talk about it; we get concerned; we make dua to recover from it quickly; people visit us; we receive get-well-soon cards.
- We never gave this a thought when we were healthy this entire time before that. Do we talk about the blessings of health during healthy times or sick times?
- Similarly, when people are rich and affluent, they never sit around talking about how much money they have or how they should be grateful to Allah for all their blessings. But when they become poor for some reason, they will start complaining and let other people know about their situation.
- Allah tests us when we have the blessings. That is the test of gratitude. Allah also tests us when we become poor. That is the test of patience and gratitude for what we have left, because there will always be people who have less than we do.

## Benefits of being grateful

- Being grateful at all times makes us healthier and happier. Over the past 20 years, researchers have found that making a habit of expressing gratitude can have significant physical and mental benefits.
- It helps us to realize how much we have in our lives that many others do not.
- It is essential for our spiritual and emotional well-being – for example, prayers are offered at times when we are grateful for something we have received.
- It relieves us of many of the pressures and anxieties we face in our daily lives.
- In times of difficulty, it helps us stay positive and thankful rather than be crushed by adverse circumstances.

وَلَقَدْ آتَيْنَا لُقْمَانَ الْحِكْمَةَ أَنِ اشْكُرْ لِلَّهِ ۚ وَمَن يَشْكُرْ فَإِنَّمَا يَشْكُرُ لِنَفْسِهِ ۖ وَمَن كَفَرَ فَإِنَّ اللَّهَ غَنِيٌّ حَمِيدٌ

"We gave Luqman wisdom and advised him to show gratitude to Allah. Anyone grateful does so to benefit his own soul, but whoever is ungrateful then verily Allah is free from all wants, and He is worthy of praise.'" (Quran 31:12)

## Quran equates ungratefulness to disbelief

- Quran equates ungratefulness with disbelief – if you are ungrateful, you are simply denying Allah, who gave you everything. This is so because you do not have any other explanation for what you have.
- Allah does not punish us even when we are ungrateful, and He continues to bestow His blessings upon us; but on the Day of Judgment, we will be questioned for this behavior.
- He is blessing those who do not believe in Him.

## Guidance from the Quran, Prophet Muhammad and Wise people

اللَّهُ الَّذِي جَعَلَ لَكُمُ اللَّيْلَ لِتَسْكُنُوا فِيهِ وَالنَّهَارَ مُبْصِرًا ۚ إِنَّ اللَّهَ لَذُو فَضْلٍ عَلَى النَّاسِ وَلَكِنَّ أَكْثَرَ النَّاسِ لَا يَشْكُرُونَ
O, people, Allah has made night dark for you so you can rest and made day bright so you can work. Indeed, Allah is very benevolent/gracious to the people, but most are not grateful. (Quran 40:61)

وَإِذْ تَأَذَّنَ رَبُّكُمْ لَئِن شَكَرْتُمْ لَأَزِيدَنَّكُمْ ۖ وَلَئِن كَفَرْتُمْ إِنَّ عَذَابِي لَشَدِيدٌ

Remember when your Lord admonished that if you are grateful, I will increase the blessings, and if you are ungrateful, then remember my punishment is severe. (Quran 31:12)

A companion asked the Prophet: "Which deed does the Almighty like the most?" He replied: "To pray on time." I asked: "Which after this?" He said, "Treating parents with kindness (due to the gratitude we owe). **(Hadith: Sahih Bukhari)**

He who does not thank people does not thank Allah". **(Hadith: Ahmad, Tirmidhi)**

Whoever does you a favor, return the favor. If you cannot find anything to return, pray for that person until you feel you have paid them back for their kindness. **(Hadith: Abu Dawood 1672)**

Some companions were by the Prophet while Umar was in his presence. The Prophet was lying on a bed of palm leaves, and beneath his head was a pillow. There wasn't any sheet between his body and the bed made of palm leaves. When he made a slight movement, it was evident that the palm leaves left a mark on his sides. Umar began crying, and the Prophet asked, "Why do you cry?" He said: "How can I not cry when I know that you are dearer to Allah than Kaiser and Caesar? Yet, they are living such lavish lives in this world". So, the Prophet said: "O Umar, wouldn't you be pleased if the Hereafter belongs to us, and this life is for them?" **(Seerah of the Prophet)**

When the Prophet prayed the night prayers, called Qiyam-ul-Layl, he would stand until his feet swelled. So, Aisha, his wife, asked: "O Prophet of Allah, do you do this whereas Allah has already forgiven you all sins/shortcomings?" He responded: "Should I not be then a grateful servant of Allah?" **(Seerah of the Prophet)**

## A Story of Sheikh Saadi

- Sheikh Saadi Shirazi traveled extensively before putting his short moral stories (called Hikayaat) on paper in the form of Gulistan (Poems) and Bostaan (Prose).

**The Man without Legs** from **Gulistan** by **Sheikh Saadi**

He faced many hardships during his travels, which he beautifully narrated in his stories. Saadi mentions that he remained patient throughout these hardships, but he arrived in a city barefoot after one particularly difficult journey. He did not have enough money to buy new shoes. With scorching heat and burning feet, a complaint to Allah came to his tongue over his present situation. He hadn't even finished his complaint while entering a mosque, and he saw a person on the street without legs dragging himself with his arms. Seeing this, Saadi humbled himself in prostration and expressed his utmost gratitude to Allah, for it is certainly better to be without shoes than without legs.

## Quick Recap

- Gratitude has been mentioned over 70 times in the Quran, where it is praised, promised a pleasant reward, prohibited, and commanded.
- Gratitude is an attitude; it takes time to develop.
- When Allah talked about His prophets in the Quran, He said they were 'grateful servants'.
- Most people are not thankful because of a lack of awareness of the blessings they have and their actualization of the essence of servitude to Allah.
- Prophet Muhammad was a grateful servant of Allah, yet it is known that when the Prophet passed away, he left neither a dinar (gold coin) nor a dirham (silver coin) in inheritance – keep in mind, he was the ruler of a Muslim land.
- Our gratitude may be enhanced by building our awareness of Allah and His sovereignty over our affairs.

# Remember,
# Blessings are a <u>test!</u>

A person can be grateful through words and actions. As a sign of gratitude to someone special, express your appreciation however you prefer. Share what you did in the next class with everyone.

# Chapter 7

# Arrogance

This chapter covers the concept of arrogance, vanity, and show-off, and why arrogance is the mother of all evils.

# The concepts

- We have discussed moral virtues so far, but arrogance is such an important concept that we should also discuss this negative trait. Eliminating arrogance can help us achieve those moral virtues.

- Let's first understand the difference between these similar words: pride, vanity, show-off, and arrogance.

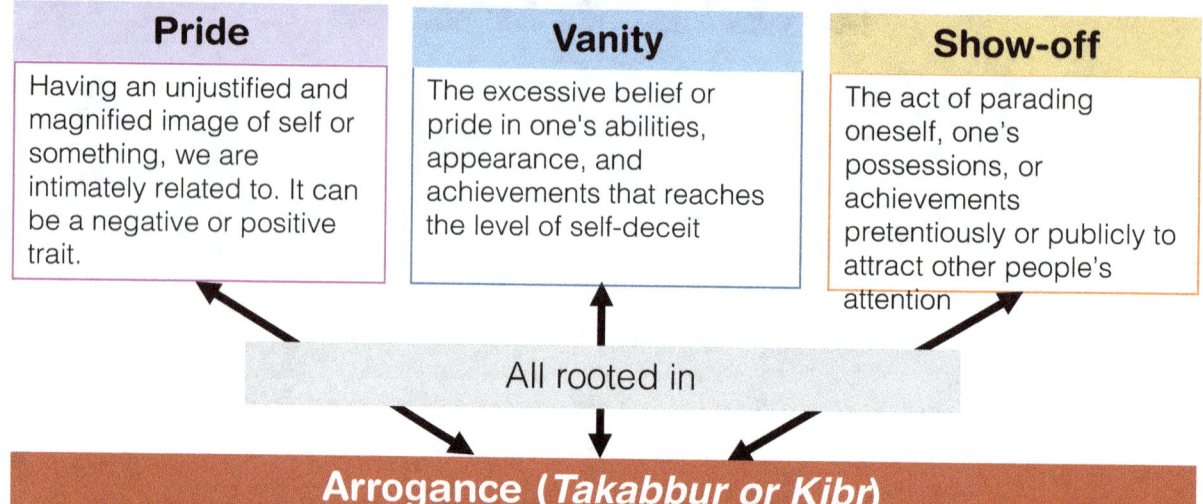

| **Pride** | **Vanity** | **Show-off** |
|---|---|---|
| Having an unjustified and magnified image of self or something, we are intimately related to. It can be a negative or positive trait. | The excessive belief or pride in one's abilities, appearance, and achievements that reaches the level of self-deceit | The act of parading oneself, one's possessions, or achievements pretentiously or publicly to attract other people's attention |

All rooted in

### Arrogance (*Takabbur or Kibr*)

Arrogance is the epitome of all these negative traits: pride, vanity, and show-off. It is the root of all evils, and an attitude of superiority and self-importance is evident in an overbearing pride. It is usually within people's hearts and is displayed in various forms.

## What is Arrogance?

- Sometimes it is difficult for us to figure out what arrogance is and how it differs from other human traits that appear to be arrogance. This is explained in one of the Ahadith by Prophet Muhammad:

Abdullah ibn Masood reported: The Prophet said, "No one who has the tiniest amount of arrogance (size of a small seed) in his heart will enter Paradise." Someone asked, "But a man loves to have beautiful clothes and shoes." The Prophet said, "Verily, Allah is beautiful, and he loves beauty. That is not arrogance. Arrogance means:

1. <u>**Rejecting the truth (which you know is the truth)**</u>
2. <u>**Look down on people (I am bigger than everyone)**</u>

# Arrogance and its signs

## Arrogance is the killer of every virtue

- In the Quran, arrogance (*Kibr*) is addressed as a foundational spiritual disease that originates from Satan and serves as a primary barrier to divine guidance.
- The reason Allah warns us about arrogance and Prophet Muhammad explained it to us is that it kills every virtue a human being can acquire. On the other hand, all evil attributes are rooted in this mother of evils.

Arrogance

No Arrogance

## Signs of Arrogance

- While we are on the journey of learning about moral character and how to develop it, we MUST stop and regularly analyze our attitude towards the truth and other people.
- Arrogance can take many forms and sneak into our personalities without us even noticing.
- Remember:
    - Arrogance blocks our path to truth.
    - It gives birth to envy and anger.
    - It's a disease, so treat it.
    - Look for symptoms.
- Let us try to rid ourselves of the tiniest amount of arrogance so it does not have a chance to grow and sprout, causing an infestation of the heart.

## Signs of Arrogance – Check yourself

- Check if you feel any of these for yourself or for others in your daily life:

- [ ] I think I am superior to others.
- [ ] My knowledge of the subject is better than the others'.
- [ ] I hate him/her regardless of what he/she says or does.
- [ ] My family background is better than his or hers.
- [ ] I think we should not meet this family because their financial status is not like ours.
- [ ] Look who is talking; I am at least more religious than you. You have no idea about religion.
- [ ] I expected that, due to my position in the organization, they would allow me to sit in the middle.
- [ ] Now, you are going to tell me what is right and what is wrong?
- [ ] I have attained this position after real hard work.
- [ ] He/She was nobody before, now he/she is telling me what to do!

I know I was wrong, but why should I accept it in front of him/her?

## Things that can make us arrogant

- The problem with arrogance is that it is a hidden disease that sometimes manifests even in what appears to be positive.
- It is well known that people become arrogant when they have power and wealth. However, many other factors in our lives can make us arrogant.
- We should be more careful about the positive things we would never imagine could be infected by the disease of arrogance.

① Knowledge　② Worship

③ Lineage　④ Leadership

⑤ Power　⑥ Beauty

⑦ Wealth

# Guidance from the Quran

إِنَّ الَّذِينَ كَذَّبُوا بِآيَاتِنَا وَاسْتَكْبَرُوا عَنْهَا لَا تُفَتَّحُ لَهُمْ أَبْوَابُ السَّمَاءِ وَلَا يَدْخُلُونَ الْجَنَّةَ

حَتَّىٰ يَلِجَ الْجَمَلُ فِي سَمِّ الْخِيَاطِ ۚ وَكَذَٰلِكَ نَجْزِي الْمُجْرِمِينَ

Indeed, those who denied Our revelations and evaded them in arrogance, the gates of heaven shall not be opened for them, nor shall they be able to enter Paradise except if a camel can pass through the eye of a needle. [This is their punishment] and thus do We punish the criminals. (Quran 7:40)

وَلَا تُصَعِّرْ خَدَّكَ لِلنَّاسِ وَلَا تَمْشِ فِي الْأَرْضِ مَرَحًا ۖ إِنَّ اللَّهَ لَا يُحِبُّ كُلَّ مُخْتَالٍ فَخُورٍ

وَاقْصِدْ فِي مَشْيِكَ وَاغْضُضْ مِن صَوْتِكَ ۚ إِنَّ أَنكَرَ الْأَصْوَاتِ لَصَوْتُ الْحَمِيرِ

And do not turn your cheeks away from people (in scorn), nor walk proudly on the earth: God does not like the arrogant and the one who expresses vanity, and be modest in your manner and keep your voice low; indeed, the most hideous of voices is the braying of the donkey. (Quran 31:18-19)

## Arrogance and Satan

وَلَقَدْ خَلَقْنَاكُمْ ثُمَّ صَوَّرْنَاكُمْ ثُمَّ قُلْنَا لِلْمَلَائِكَةِ اسْجُدُوا لِآدَمَ فَسَجَدُوا إِلَّا إِبْلِيسَ لَمْ يَكُن مِّنَ السَّاجِدِينَ

قَالَ مَا مَنَعَكَ أَلَّا تَسْجُدَ إِذْ أَمَرْتُكَ ۖ قَالَ أَنَا خَيْرٌ مِّنْهُ خَلَقْتَنِي مِن نَّارٍ وَخَلَقْتَهُ مِن طِينٍ

And indeed, We created you all, and We then fashioned you. Then we said to the Angels (and Jinns) to prostrate to Adam, and they all did except Iblees, who did not. God said what stopped you from prostration when I commanded it. Iblees said, "I am better than him. You have created me from fire, and You have created him from dust/clay". (Quran 7:11-12)

- Satan is an adjective that can be applied to a Jinn or a human being.
- Iblees (Satan) was a Jinn who refused to obey God, even though he knew God first-hand and God talked to him directly.
- The attribute that made him bold enough to disobey God was **arrogance** (this shows how dangerous arrogance can be).
- He disobeyed God and doomed himself eternally to hellfire merely for the fact that he was created from a better form of matter than a human being.
- This whole concept of 'superiority' over other creations or human beings pushes us toward arrogance.
- When it comes to gaining the right knowledge or knowing the right thing, our attitude MUST be far from Satan's.

## Healthy vs Negative pride

- Pride can be a positive force that pushes us to do things that we cannot achieve otherwise. However, we have to be careful when it becomes negative and manifests as arrogance.
- According to Psychology Today, here are the differences between positive and negative pride.

### Positive Pride

- It develops self-confidence, reflecting a motivating "can-do" attitude.
- I am not that good, but if I work a little harder, I can improve.
- I am working hard, and I think I will be able to do it, but don't tell anyone this because I am not certain how I will perform.
- I will try my best, but I don't think I am good at this.
- If I can do it, anyone can.

### Negative Pride

- I want to do something to show them that I can do it too.
- I did an incredible job compared to others, but I was not treated fairly.
- Guys, don't be surprised if we win the game. We are going to crush you.
- Only I can do it; I would not recommend you try this.
- I am surprised that he/she could even achieve this.

## The story of Qaroon in the Quran

- The Qaroon lived in the time of Musa and was considered the symbol of arrogance, pride, and show-off.
- He had so much wealth that the keys to his treasure were once carried by many strong men.
- This extraordinary wealth and treasure made him arrogant and insolent toward other people.
- He attributed all his wealth to his knowledge and wisdom, without realizing that it was a test from God.
- Sometimes God punishes people in this world when they grow arrogant and rude to such an extent that God wants to teach them a lesson for the benefit of others and future generations.
- According to the Quran, God punished him by instructing the earth to swallow him and his wealth (in his house) with no rescue. People who saw this ending realized that God gives all the blessings, and we have no right to become arrogant about that.

## Show off – its dangers

- Often, people think of showing off as an innocent act, but it quickly becomes dangerous.
- In Islam, showing off in religious matters is even considered **Minor Shirk**.
- All our worship MUST be done purely for the sake of God, with no intention of seeking admiration from others.
- Feeling good about oneself, a good name, a reputation, and admiration are natural urges – we have to keep a check on them and make sure we do not trip on the other side.
- These urges are used the most by Satan.
- No intelligent person would want to waste their efforts and energy on something that does not bring them any reward and instead earns them sins.
- People who like to show off are usually self-centered, and they want everything to revolve around them.
- When we do something good (prayer or helping someone), we should not seek admiration; instead, we should seek encouragement.
- The most dangerous thing about show-off and the pride associated with it is that the person involved in it won't see this behavior as a problem.

> The disease that knowledge brings is arrogance, and the disease that worship brings is showing off. (Ibn Taymiyyah)

## Guidance from Prophet's Best Example

"Verily, what I fear most for you is the *minor shirk*." And he elaborated, "It is showing off. Allah SWT will say to them (who show off), on the Day of Resurrection, when the people are being rewarded for their deeds: Go to those whom you wished to show off in the world and look for your reward with them." (Hadith: Musnad Ahmad 23119)

The Prophet said, He who lets people hear of his good deeds intentionally, to win their praise, Allah will let the people know his real intention (on the Day of Resurrection), and he who does good things in public to show off and win the praise of the people, Allah will disclose his real intention (and humiliate him). (Hadith: Sahih Bukhari 6499)

## How to avoid arrogance, pride, and show off

Completely removing arrogance and pride in any shape or form is a tough task. However, we must try our best. These are some practical tips:

1. Hide your good deeds – occasionally, you want to share with others, only to encourage them.
2. Look at the message, not the messenger.
3. Don't get angry when someone criticizes you – criticism can be healthy or unhealthy.
4. Always ask for advice and feedback on anything you do – even if you think you have done the best job.
5. Talk about things, characteristics, behavior, attributes, and issues, but not about specific people.
6. Always remember that whatever you have is a blessing from God, and He deserves all the praise and thanks for it.
7. If you are good at something, always be grateful to God for the talent or capability you have, by taking the name of that capability.
8. Share your knowledge, wealth, and time with others.
9. Avoid argumentation even when you know you are right and the other person is wrong.
10. If you have bad feelings about someone, make dua for them and give them a gift.
11. If you have hurt someone's feelings, ask for forgiveness and make amends.

## Quick Recap

- Pride, vanity, and show off all stem from arrogance or lead to arrogance – BEWARE.
- Arrogance is rejecting the truth and despising people.
- Remember this hadith: No one will enter paradise whose heart is a mustard seed of arrogance.
- Arrogance is Satan's biggest trap (he wants to avenge his doom to hell).
- Satan, despite knowing God personally, could not resist the temptation of arrogance.
- Arrogance can take many forms and sneak into our personalities without us noticing.
- It gives birth to envy and anger.
- Treat arrogance like a disease.
- Look for symptoms and eliminate them as quickly as possible.
- Showing off our good deeds will get us NOTHING in the DoJ – that's not smart.

# Remember,

*Arrogance, vanity, pride, and show-off are hidden diseases; we need to carefully look for their symptoms every day and get rid of them.*

- What are some examples of vanity and show-off that you've experienced in your daily life?
- Are there things that look like arrogance and show-off but aren't?

# Chapter 8

# Justice

This chapter covers the concept of justice, which is central to the Quran's teaching.

# The concept of Justice

- The word justice is usually construed as something done in the courtroom or at the king or ruler level, and never related to a common man and his/her daily life or this universe.
- In philosophy and law, justice means fairness, equality, and moral rightness.
- But justice, really, means "giving each their due".
- In Arabic, the generic word for justice is *Adl or Qist*. It creates the balance needed for everything to function perfectly. If it is not maintained, everything becomes disturbed and unbalanced.

**Justice** means *placing things in their rightful place*

- Allah maintains that balance in the universe and His teachings, and He insists that we maintain that balance too:

وَالسَّمَاءَ رَفَعَهَا وَوَضَعَ الْمِيزَانَ ۝ أَلَّا تَطْغَوْا فِي الْمِيزَانِ ۝ وَأَقِيمُوا الْوَزْنَ بِالْقِسْطِ وَلَا تُخْسِرُوا الْمِيزَانَ

And He raised high the heavens and set the scale of all things (balanced) that you [also in your circle of authority] do not transgress that scale. Give just weight and full measure. (Quran 55:7-9)

- An example of the balance Allah created can be found in our complex universe.
- In Science, the gravitational constant G determines the strength of the gravitational force between two masses. If G were altered slightly, it would have huge effects on the universe:
  - If G were slightly stronger, Stars would burn much hotter and faster. This could drastically shorten their lifespans, reducing the time available for life to develop and evolve.
  - If G were slightly weaker, Stars would burn cooler and more slowly, which could affect their ability to sustain nuclear fusion and form heavy elements. This might lead to a universe with fewer, less diverse stars, which in turn could affect the formation of planets and the potential for life.

# Justice in Islam

- In Islam, justice starts with you and me before it applies to the court or ruler.
- We praise justice because justice is an attribute of Allah, and for this reason, its likeness has been ordained in our nature – this is a universal concept within humanity.
- Justice is a personal virtue and one of the standards of moral excellence that a believer is encouraged to attain as part of his God-consciousness.
- A small 'court of justice' is within every person, which delivers unbiased verdicts at all times.
- Justice becomes more important when it concerns people who are less fortunate, more vulnerable, or are under your care – be careful in dealing with them.
- One form of justice is to give the position to someone capable of taking it.

## Allah's stress on Justice

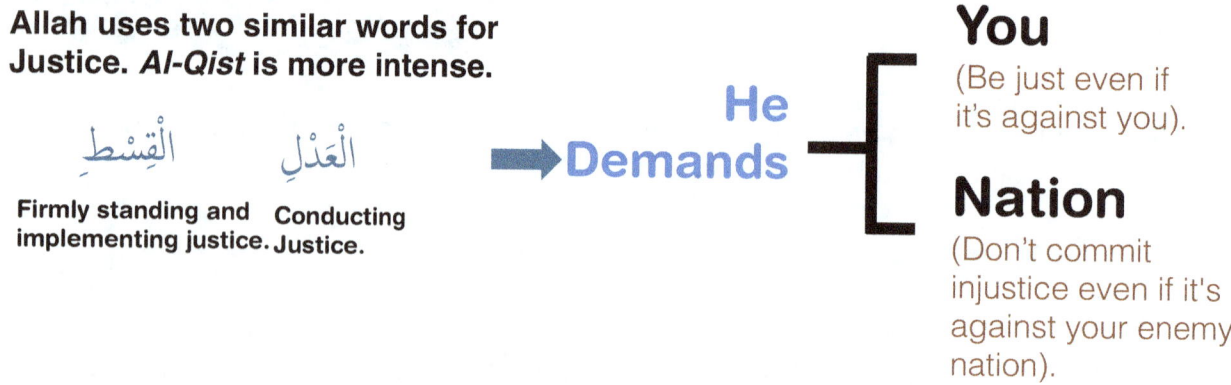

**Allah uses two similar words for Justice. *Al-Qist* is more intense.**

الْقِسْطِ     الْعَدْلِ

**Firmly standing and implementing justice.**   **Conducting Justice.**

**He ➡ Demands**

**You**
(Be just even if it's against you).

**Nation**
(Don't commit injustice even if it's against your enemy nation).

- The Quran made justice the necessary outcome and mandatory requirement of faith in the heart – a seed properly sown and taken care of will always bear fruit.
- A person committing injustices lacks faith in Allah.
- We are not asked to be just once, but we must be among those who uphold justice throughout our lives.
- The Quran demands that we avoid even the slightest injustice against anyone.
- Allah wants us to stand up and adhere to justice to become a witness on the day of judgment, where we will have to testify against/for our actions.
- Allah has asked us to be just with orphans because they are most vulnerable to injustice.
- He revealed Scriptures/Books for one purpose: to guide people on the path of justice in religion.
- The day of judgment will occur for one reason: **to serve justice.**

يَا أَيُّهَا الَّذِينَ آمَنُوا كُونُوا قَوَّامِينَ بِالْقِسْطِ شُهَدَاءَ لِلَّهِ وَلَوْ عَلَى أَنْفُسِكُمْ أَوِ الْوَالِدَيْنِ وَالْأَقْرَبِينَ ۚ إِنْ يَكُنْ غَنِيًّا أَوْ فَقِيرًا فَاللَّهُ أَوْلَىٰ بِهِمَا ۖ فَلَا تَتَّبِعُوا الْهَوَىٰ أَنْ تَعْدِلُوا ۚ وَإِنْ تَلْوُوا أَوْ تُعْرِضُوا فَإِنَّ اللَّهَ كَانَ بِمَا تَعْمَلُونَ خَبِيرًا

Believers! Adhere to justice by bearing witness to it for Allah, even though it be against **yourselves**, your parents, or your kinsfolk. If someone is rich or poor, Allah is more worthy of both. So do not be led by base desires [by leaving His guidance], lest, as a result, you swerve from the truth. And if you distort [what is true and just] or evade [it, you should remember that], Allah is well aware of what you do. (Quran 4:135)

يَا أَيُّهَا الَّذِينَ آمَنُوا كُونُوا قَوَّامِينَ لِلَّهِ شُهَدَاءَ بِالْقِسْطِ ۖ وَلَا يَجْرِمَنَّكُمْ شَنَآنُ قَوْمٍ عَلَىٰ أَلَّا تَعْدِلُوا ۚ اعْدِلُوا هُوَ أَقْرَبُ لِلتَّقْوَىٰ ۖ وَاتَّقُوا اللَّهَ ۚ إِنَّ اللَّهَ خَبِيرٌ بِمَا تَعْمَلُونَ

Believers! Be those who adhere to justice by bearing witness to it for Allah. And your animosity for some **people/nation** should not induce you to turn away from justice. Be just; this is nearer to piety. And have a fear of Allah; indeed, Allah is well aware of all your deeds. (Quran 5:8)

## Adhering to Justice is hard

- Adhering to justice at all times is an uphill battle.
- It requires inner strength because it may involve people whom you love or have an affiliation with who may be committing injustice, and you have to stand against it.
- The weaknesses that usually affect our notion of justice are: emotions, cowardice, vested interest, biases, and relationships.
- Sometimes, you will have to pay the price for adhering to justice.
- On the day of judgment, our attitude and actions towards justice will be of great importance before Allah – we will have to justify our decisions and actions.
- The Quran is very explicit about the importance of justice in our personal lives.

In Islam, we believe in the Day of Judgement because of the ultimate justice it will serve. But many people do not believe in it. What arguments can one have against such a day?

# Guidance from the Quran and the Prophet's Examples

- As we saw before, the Quran instructs believers to stand firm for justice, even if it goes against themselves, their parents, or their friends.

- Imagine your best friend cheats on a test. Justice means not lying to the teacher to cover for them, even though you love your friend. Standing up for what is right is more important than "loyalty" to a wrong action.

- Even if someone gets away with injustice in this world, the Quran promises that Allah is all-watching and that perfect justice will be served in the afterlife.

- It is also just to give the responsibilities to the people in charge who are capable of fulfilling those responsibilities. This eliminates the threat of nepotism, which destroys societies.

إِنَّ اللَّهَ يَأْمُرُ بِالْعَدْلِ

Indeed, Allah commands justice. (Quran 16:90)

إِنَّ اللَّهَ يَأْمُرُكُمْ أَن تُؤَدُّوا الْأَمَانَاتِ إِلَى أَهْلِهَا وَإِذَا حَكَمْتُم بَيْنَ النَّاسِ أَن تَحْكُمُوا بِالْعَدْلِ ۚ إِنَّ اللَّهَ نِعِمَّا يَعِظُكُم بِهِ ۗ إِنَّ اللَّهَ كَانَ سَمِيعًا بَصِيرًا

"Allah commands you to render trusts to whom they are due, and when you judge between people, judge with justice. This is excellent advice from Allah. Indeed, Allah is All-hearing, All-seeing ..." (Quran 4:58)

There are seven categories of people whom Allah will shelter under His shade on the Day when there will be no shade except His.  One of them will be a just leader." (Hadith: Sahih Muslim)

"O My slaves, I have forbidden injustice for Myself and forbade it also for you. So avoid being unjust to one another." (Hadith-e-Qudsi: Sahih Muslim)

Verily, those who deal with fairness will be in the presence of Allah upon pulpits of light, near the right hand of the Merciful, the Exalted, and both of His sides are right (being equal in honor); those who practiced justice in their rulings and with their families and in all that they did. (Hadith: Sahih Muslim 4493)

# Injustice (The Darkness)

- The lack of justice is called injustice. However, it may take a severe form if the person begins committing evil against others.
- The Quran introduced the unique concept that committing injustice to others, including Allah, and/or sinning in general, is actually committing injustice to your own soul, because the person committing injustice will bear the consequences in the end.

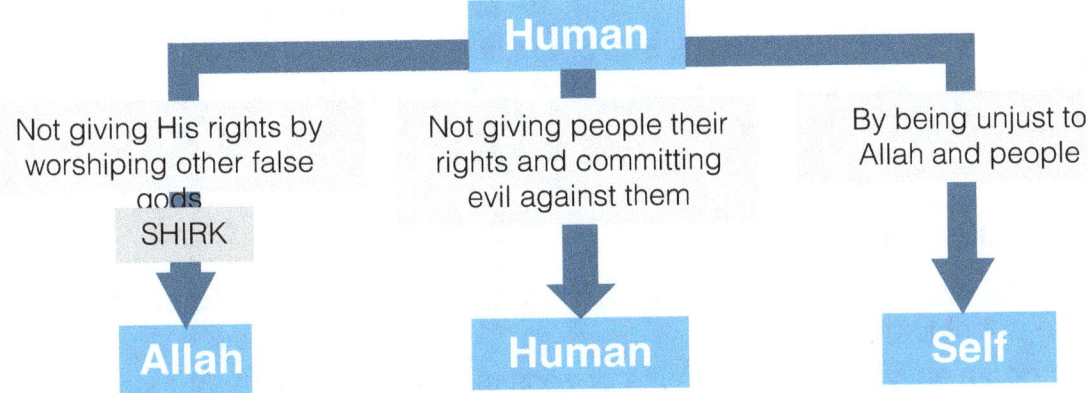

- Any form of injustice in a society leads to the following and more.

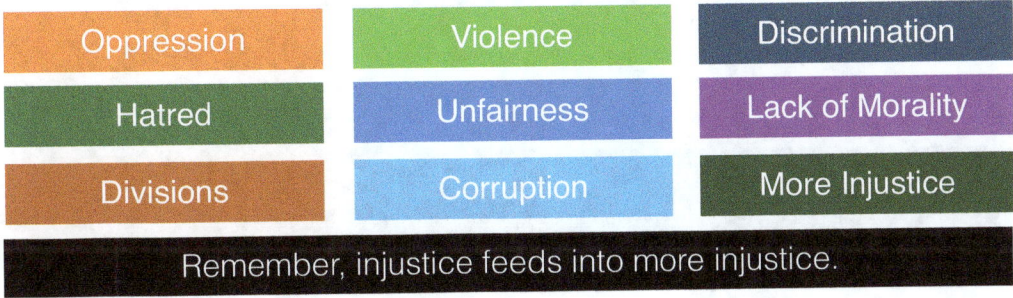

## How to respond to Injustice

- Injustice should be handled with wisdom.
- Justice requires that you are fully aware of the events and situation, and must hear both sides if there are two people/parties involved.
- 'Standing up' for justice should be according to your understanding of the situation, relative position, power, relationship, etc. Standing up for justice can mean any of these:

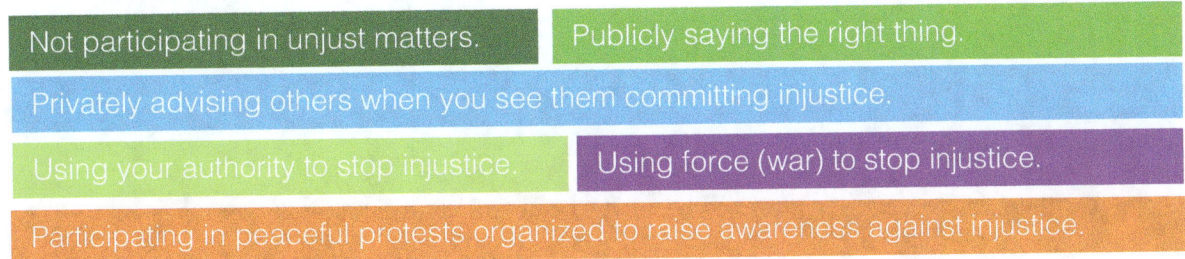

## Guidance from Prophet's Best Example

Guard yourself against oppression, for oppression will be darkness on the Day of Resurrection. Guard yourself against greed, for it has destroyed those who came before you. It caused them to shed blood and to make lawful what was unlawful. (Hadith: Sahih Muslim 2578)

Beware of the supplication of the oppressed, even if he is an unbeliever, for there is no screen between it and Allah. (Hadith: Masnad Ahmad 12140)

"Help your brother, whether he is an oppressor or an oppressed one. People asked, "O Allah's Messenger, it is all right to help him if he is oppressed, but how should we help him if he is an oppressor?" The Prophet said, "By preventing him from oppressing others." (Hadith: Sahih Al-Bukhari 2444)

## Justice, justice, justice …

- We face many situations in our lives every day, and we don't realize that they require upholding justice.
- Justice is an active choice we make dozens of times a day without realizing it.
- We should be careful when making choices in situations where Allah wants us to uphold justice. Whether it's in our school, in our house, or in the group chat we're in on social media.

| Situation 1 | Situation 2 |
|---|---|
| I noticed that my best friend is involved in bullying a new student in the school. | You need to choose between your friend and another student for a group project, in which the other student is a better pick. |

| Situation 3 | Situation 4 |
|---|---|
| My brother is involved in a fight at school that he started, and the principal called me as a witness to determine who was responsible. | This is Eid time, and with the little money that I have, I am figuring out who I should buy a gift for, my mom or my best friend. |

**Remember, Justice means placing things in their rightful place.**

## Quick Recap

- Justice is the most important virtue that Allah wants us to develop in our character – it is fundamental and impacts our other traits.
- In Islam, the concept of justice starts with you and me before it applies to the court or ruler.
- The concept of justice is ingrained in us as part of our moral being.
- Justice is one of the mandatory requirements of faith in Allah.
- The day of judgment will occur only to serve justice.
- The weaknesses that usually affect our notion of justice are: emotions, cowardice, vested interest, biases, and relationships.
- Injustice leads to many vices in society and drags society toward destruction.
- We should handle injustice with wisdom.

Suggest how we can be just to the environment around us and, as a result, reduce our impact on other human beings or the environment. Share it with the class next week.

# Chapter 9

# Courage

This chapter covers the concept of courage, which is often misunderstood as the absence of fear. The greatest and most difficult type of courage is moral courage.

# The concept of Courage

- Courage is often misunderstood as "having no fear." Fear and courage exist together.
- Courage means that fear should not hold you back from doing the right thing that you are supposed to do.
- Fearless means not allowing fear to take over.
- Generally, courage is also called bravery.
- Courage, in general, is a good virtue, but it is NOT just about trying new things, climbing heights, facing dangers, etc. – a critical aspect of courage is acting for moral reasons.
- Showing determination to respect the limits set by God without hesitation, and to fear none but God, requires moral courage.

**Courage is an attitude and not a one-time thing.**

The only thing necessary for the success of evil is that good men and women do nothing.
(Anonymous)

## Moral Courage

- As a virtue, courage means acting for moral reasons despite the risk of unpleasant consequences.
- Moral courage is closely related to truthfulness, honesty, and justice.
- A person can be very "courageous" in the presence of physical danger, but he/she may not have the moral courage to make the right choices.
- Moral courage is required when you must choose between right and wrong, and between good and bad – it requires conviction in moral principles.

## Courage in our words and actions

- In Islam, as with many other virtues, courage is founded on a strong faith in God and on our sincerity in that faith.
- It is unconditional belief in the fact that if we are courageous enough to say the right thing, make the right choices, or do the right thing, then God's support and help will be with us.
- Not every situation requires us to display courage through actions – it is enough to speak the truth with courage.
- There is a difference between "courage" and "boldness" – boldness means saying or doing anything that the person's mind is thinking (remember, it may have negative consequences).
- The virtue of courage should be used with wisdom – courage shown out of emotional feelings, without thinking, may produce negative results.

## Demonstration of courage

- Don't limit courage to being fearless or outspoken; courage is required and can be demonstrated in many ways:
    - Accepting our mistakes, faults, and failures requires a lot of courage.
    - Trying something that you know you are not good at, but you need to do it as circumstances demand it – getting out of your comfort zone.
    - Having self-control at times when you are extremely angry.
    - Holding ourselves at times when we know saying the right thing may make things worse.
    - Holding ourselves at times when we are provoked, and we know we can handle it with force.
    - Listening to and heeding someone's advice, or learning from someone who may be younger than us or lower in position or rank, keeping your ego aside.
    - Accepting calamities and tragedies of life with patience, knowing that it is the decree of God.
    - Avoiding feelings of regret, doubt, and fear of consequences after making a thoughtful decision.
    - Forgiving others while knowing they have hurt you.

We have learned many ways to demonstrate courage; share your life stories or events in which you demonstrated courage using one of those means.

## Guidance from the Quran and Prophet's best examples

The Quran mentions the story of the people of the cave in Surah Kahf. Surah Kahf is named after the story it tells. They were young men who demonstrated the moral courage to remain steadfast in their belief that God is one and alone, with no partners. They showed the courage to speak the truth, even when they were an oppressed minority in a city with a tyrant king. They used their courage wisely at that time and found refuge in a cave while refusing to accept their polytheistic beliefs. (Surah Kahf)

Whosoever of you sees an evil, let him change it with his hand; and if he is not able to do so, then [let him change it] with his tongue; and if he is not able to do so, then with his heart — and that is the weakest of faith. (Hadith: Sahih Muslim) (See Note)

**Note:** *This hadith applies only to situations in which someone has the authority and control to do so. For example, if the head of a family perceives evil in their household and fails to address it out of fear, love, or other factors, they are at a lower level of faith. As a family head, he should have the moral courage to control evil.*

لَّقَدْ كَانَ لَكُمْ فِي رَسُولِ اللَّهِ أُسْوَةٌ حَسَنَةٌ

Indeed, in the Messenger of Allah, you have a great example to follow. (Quran 33:21)

> **Note:** *In the Battle of the Trenches (also called Ahzab), the forces of the idolatrous Arabs and the Jews were mobilized against Islam, and after forming a strong military alliance, they besieged Medinah for about one month. As various tribes and groups participated in this battle and the Muslims dug a ditch around Medinah to counter the enemy's advances, the situation was dire for the Muslims. At that moment, God commended Prophet Muhammad's courage and resolved the situation.*

A strong man is not someone good at wrestling (physical fighting), but he is the one who controls himself in a fit of rage. (Hadith: Al-Bukhari and Muslim)

A man said to the Prophet, 'Give me advice.' The Prophet said, "Do not get angry." The man asked the same question three times, and the Prophet answered each time, "Do not get angry." (Hadith: Al-Bukhari and Muslim)

The Prophet has said, after seeing two people arguing and angry at one another: "I know a word which, if you were to say it, what you feel would go away; you need to say 'I seek refuge with Allah from the Satan' (*A'audhu Billah e Min Ash-Shaytan Ar Rajeem*) and all his anger would go away." (Hadith: Sahih Bukhari 6, 337)

A man asked the Prophet when he was about to ride his horse: "Which kind of Jihad or fighting is the best?" He said: "A word of truth spoken in front of an unjust ruler." (Hadith: An-Nisai)

When Prophet Muhammad decided to migrate to Medinah, he took Abu Bakr with him, and they set out. The people of Makkah, his enemies, sent people after them to trace them down. At one point, while hiding in a small cave, as enemies approached very close to them and were about to find them, Abu Bakr felt unsafe and told the Prophet they might get caught. At that moment, Prophet Muhammad responded, "Do not grieve, God is with us." (Seerah of Prophet Muhammad)

The prophet was quick at facing danger. One night, the people of Medinah heard a strange noise that frightened them. Some people set out toward the sound when they saw the Messenger of Allah already on his way back after investigating the source of the noise. He was riding an unsaddled horse belonging to Abu Talha, and a sword was hanging around his neck, and he was saying: "Do not be afraid! Do not be afraid!" (Hadith: Sahih Al-Bukhari and Muslim)

## Quick Recap

- Courage and fear exist together - courage means that fear should not hold you back from doing the right thing, which you are supposed to do.
- Moral courage is closely related to truthfulness, honesty, and justice.
- Have a solid unconditional belief in the fact that if we are courageous enough to say the right thing, make the right choices, or do the right thing, then God's support and help will be with us.
- The virtue of courage should be used with wisdom.
- We should not limit courage to being fearless or outspoken; courage is required and can be demonstrated in many ways.
- Controlling your anger during a fit of rage is a courageous act that most people cannot demonstrate.
- Sometimes, our comfortable lives make us weak and cowardly – It is always good to get out of our comfort zone to be courageous.
- We should teach the quality of courage in the face of our fears and, more importantly, courage as a moral value.

1. Is it courageous to fight a bully in your school?
2. Are there occasions where demonstrating courage would be harmful?

# Chapter 10

## Mercy

This chapter covers the concept of mercy that encompasses this universe, wherever we see it. However, it's a concept related to both Allah and human beings.

# The concept of Mercy

- Mercy is the compassion and forbearance shown towards people who have either offended us or are weak (orphans, destitute) or are under our authority (lower in rank, age, or power).
- The Arabic word for Mercy, **Rahmah**, is derived from the root word for mother's womb – there is nothing more merciful than the mother's womb for an unborn child.
- However, the mercy of God differs slightly from that of human beings. Mercy is the most frequently mentioned attribute of God in the Quran – 113 Surahs out of 114 start with "**Bismillah Ar-Rahman Ar-Raheem**."
- Mercy is one of God's attributes, and He bestowed it on us when He created us.
- God is merciful to all His creations, regardless of their behavior.
- Mercy is something ingrained in us; it exists even in the wildest of animals, like lions.
- Showing mercy to others brings joy and happiness to our hearts.
- Mercy is often desired in mutual relationships and in spreading love in society.

Islam is often misrepresented as the "religion of violence," which lacks mercy towards other human beings. Some verses of the Quran, taken out of context, and the behavior of a small minority are the main reasons behind this.

## God's attributes of Mercy

### Ar-Raheem الرَّحِيْم

The quality of Mercy that makes it work all the time with permanence, not just one time.

### Ar-Rahman الرَّحْمٰن

The quality of Mercy that makes it too intense and want to be visible everywhere.

- If we look at ourselves and around us, all we see is God's mercy – our bodies, health, families, food, rain, rivers, mountains, oceans, skies, wind, trees, and plants… every blessing is a result of God's mercy.
- However, the concept of Mercy as an attribute of God differs slightly from its application to human beings.
- God's Mercy has Justice embedded in it. His act of Justice is the result of His Mercy, or in other words, His Mercy demands that He must be Just also.
- On the Day of Judgment, His Mercy will have the component of Justice in it.

كَتَبَ عَلَى نَفْسِهِ الرَّحْمَةَ لَيَجْمَعَنَّكُمْ اِلٰى يَوْمِ الْقِيٰمَةِ لَا رَيْبَ فِيْهِ

He has made Mercy mandatory on Himself. So definitely, He shall take all of you towards the Day of Judgement and gather all of you on that day, for which there is no doubt. (Quran 6:12)

وَرَحْمَتِي وَسِعَتْ كُلَّ شَيْءٍ

And My Mercy encompasses everything. (Quran 7:156)

كَتَبَ رَبُّكُمْ عَلَى نَفْسِهِ الرَّحْمَةَ أَنَّهُ مَنْ عَمِلَ مِنكُمْ سُوءًا بِجَهَالَةٍ ثُمَّ تَابَ مِن بَعْدِهِ وَأَصْلَحَ فَأَنَّهُ غَفُورٌ رَّحِيمٌ

Your Lord has made mercy incumbent upon Himself. So, whoever did something evil out of ignorance or emotions and then repented and corrected it, then He is most forgiving, the merciful. (Quran 7:156)

- Prophet Muhammad has told us about God's mercy in this beautiful hadith:

Of a hundred parts of mercy, one part is the mercy with which the creation is merciful between themselves, and ninety-nine parts are for God for the Day of Resurrection.
(Hadith: Sahih Muslim 2753)

## Receiving mercy from God

- We all need mercy from God in this world and the Hereafter – we can't enter paradise just because of our deeds.
- The best way to earn God's mercy is to show mercy toward His creation.
- We should strive to develop humility in ourselves. Humility is an internal feeling of a person that makes him/her submit before God and produces in him/her the feelings of mercy and love for other human beings.
- In this world, God shows mercy to everyone, whether we believe in Him or not, obey Him or not. On the day of judgment, His mercy will be restricted to those who seek Him and His mercy.
- If God extends His mercy to criminals on the day of judgment, then He won't be just.

## Who deserves our mercy?

- We are asked to be merciful to the destitute, orphans, and people who are under our authority.
- In our home, people who deserve our mercy the most are our younger siblings and pets (if we have them).
- In old age, our parents and grandparents deserve our mercy most of all.
- We are required to show mercy not only toward other human beings but also toward animals, the environment, and the surroundings.
- Showing mercy towards each other (peers) creates an environment of love and care.

- There are many ways we can show mercy towards others:
  - Be patient with other people's irritating behavior.
  - Don't hold people accountable immediately; give them a second, maybe a third, chance.
  - Respond politely to your younger siblings when they ask the same thing repeatedly.
  - Be good to those who may have hurt you.
  - Visit the sick and the people who are suffering financially or emotionally.
  - Make dua for the people who may have hurt you.

وَقَضَىٰ رَبُّكَ أَلَّا تَعْبُدُوا إِلَّا إِيَّاهُ وَبِالْوَالِدَيْنِ إِحْسَانًا ۚ إِمَّا يَبْلُغَنَّ عِندَكَ الْكِبَرَ أَحَدُهُمَا أَوْ كِلَاهُمَا فَلَا تَقُل لَّهُمَا أُفٍّ وَلَا تَنْهَرْهُمَا وَقُل لَّهُمَا قَوْلًا كَرِيمًا وَاخْفِضْ لَهُمَا جَنَاحَ الذُّلِّ مِنَ الرَّحْمَةِ وَقُل رَّبِّ ارْحَمْهُمَا كَمَا رَبَّيَانِي صَغِيرًا

And [remember that] your Lord has enjoined you to worship none but Him, and to treat well your parents. If either or both of them attain old age in your life before you, show them no sign of impatience, nor scold them while answering; but speak to them with good etiquette and lower your wings of humility from mercy for them and say: "Lord, be merciful to them the way they nursed me in childhood. " (Quran 17:23-24)

## Prophet Muhammad is the Prophet of Mercy

- Prophet Muhammad is called the Prophet of mercy because of the message that he brought to humanity and how he acted throughout his life as a Messenger.
- The way he led his life is a testament to his true Messengerhood.
- When the mother of the believers, Aisha, was asked about his character, she said that his character was the Quran, as the Quran is a mercy to all humanity, like him.

وَمَا أَرْسَلْنَاكَ إِلَّا رَحْمَةً لِّلْعَالَمِينَ

O Messenger, We have not sent you but as a mercy to the worlds. (Quran: 21:107)

The Messenger of Allah was asked, "O Messenger of Allah, pray against the idolaters!" So, the Prophet said: Verily, I was not sent to invoke curses, but rather I was only sent as a mercy. (Hadith: Sahih Muslim 2599)

## Guidance from the Quran and the Prophet's life

Allah does not show mercy to those who do not show mercy to people. (Hadith: Al-Bukhari and Muslim)

Those who show mercy will be shown mercy by the Merciful [Lord]. Show mercy to those on earth, and He Who is in the heavens will show mercy to you. (Hadith: Al-Tirmidhi)

Once, a woman searched for her boy until she suddenly found him among the captives. She pulled him to her stomach and breastfed him, at which point the Prophet said, "Do you think this woman would throw her child into a fire?" We said, "No, O Messenger of Allah, not while she cannot throw him." The Prophet said, "Allah is certainly more merciful with His servants than this woman is with her child." (Hadith: Sahih Bukhari 5653)

You will never truly have faith until you love one another. Shall I tell you what will make you love each other? They said, "Of course, O Messenger of Allah." The Prophet said: Spread peace among yourselves. By the one in whose hand is my soul, you will not enter Paradise until you are merciful. (Hadith: Al-Mustadrak 7391)

Once, the Prophet was asked about a woman who locked up a cat and did not feed her until she died, and the Prophet responded that the woman would be thrown in hellfire as she had no mercy in her heart. (Seerah of Prophet Muhammad)

When the Prophet visited *Ta'if* to preach the message of Islam, he was ridiculed, tortured, and pushed out of the city. Angel Jibrael gave him a choice of punishing the people of *Ta'if* by crushing the city between two mountains, and the prophet said, No, I hope that God will bring out from their offspring people who worship Him alone and associate no partners with Him. (Seerah of Prophet Muhammad)

When Prophet Muhammad conquered Makkah after living away from his birthplace for more than 9 years, he forgave everyone in the city and took no revenge despite the fact that the very same people persecuted him, tried to kill him, and forced him to migrate to another land. (Seerah of Prophet Muhammad)

Once, a Bedouin entered the Prophet's mosque for the first time. He said, supplicating, "O Allah, forgive Muhammad and me, but don't forgive anyone else!" The Prophet smiled at him and remarked gently, "You are limiting Allah's forgiveness, which is vast." Later, the man urinated on the masjid floor. The Prophet calmed the upset onlookers and told them to leave the man alone and let him finish his task. He reminded his companions that they were sent to make things easier for people, not more difficult. The Bedouin later recounted his experience with the Prophet: May my mother and father be sacrificed for him. He did not scold or insult me. He just said, 'We do not urinate in these mosques-they were built for prayer and remembrance of Allah.' Then, he called for a bucket of water to be poured on the ground. (Seerah of Prophet Muhammad)

- If we look at ourselves and around us, all we see is mercy from God – our body, health, family, food, rain, rivers, mountains, oceans, skies, wind, trees, and plants ….. Every blessing is the result of God's mercy.
- Islam is often misrepresented as the "religion of violence," which lacks mercy toward other human beings – it is our responsibility to correct this impression.
- The best way to earn God's mercy is to show mercy toward His creation.
- In our home, people who deserve our mercy the most are our younger siblings, pets (if we have them), and older parents/grandparents.
- There are many ways we can show mercy toward others.
- We have many lessons from the life of Prophet Muhammad on how to be merciful to our fellow beings.
- Having mercy in our mutual relationships creates an environment of love and care.

- If you are asked to demonstrate mercy in your life, what acts would you do to show that?
- How can you be merciful and just at the same time?

- Write a small essay with examples that convince non-Muslims that Islam is a religion of peace and mercy.

# Chapter 11

# Truthfulness

This chapter covers the concept of truthfulness, which is one of those attributes that leaves a lasting impact on others if you consistently practice it.

# The concept of Truthfulness

 **"The biggest advantage of being truthful is that you don't have to remember what you said."**

- Truthfulness is all about telling the truth or stating the facts correctly to the best of our knowledge in front of other people – closely related to honesty.
- Truthfulness is so important in the eyes of God that when He introduced many of His Prophets in the Quran, He called them "truthful prophets".
- Prophet Muhammad was known among his people as "As-Sadiq (Truthful)" and "Al-Amin (Trustworthy)" even before his prophethood.
- Truthfulness is ingrained in us and is a universal trait that brings tranquility and peace to our hearts, and our conscience always remains satisfied.
- However, unfortunately, finding truthfulness in today's world is the hardest thing.
- Being truthful is not easy – it may bring temporary trouble and loss (it requires moral courage).

## Source of many virtues

- Being truthful is the source of many righteous deeds – in other words, avoiding lying may stop you from committing bad deeds.
- Truthfulness is larger than the action of the tongue. The outside should be what's inside. Actions must be based on the belief, and you should preach with practice.
- Truthfulness is something that needs to be cultivated until it reflects through our character.
- Truthfulness is the seed of the best of morals.

One of the best ways we can acquire the quality of truthfulness is to remain in the company of truthful people.

# A believer is a personification of Truthfulness

## The Quran's demand for Truthfulness

يَا أَيُّهَا الَّذِينَ آمَنُوا اتَّقُوا اللَّهَ وَكُونُوا مَعَ الصَّادِقِينَ

Believers, fear Allah and be with the truthful. (Quran 9:119)

- Truthfulness is required at all times in every aspect of our lives.
- In the Quran, many verses that command us to be truthful begin with "fear Allah" – truthfulness is one of the manifestations of the consciousness of Allah (also called Taqwa).
- The Quran gives truthfulness such high regard that it promises those who adhere to it to be with the prophets and martyrs in Paradise.
- Truthfulness demands that we talk 'straight' when telling the truth – it does not mean we should be disrespectful.
- Not only should we be truthful in our speech, but we should also accept and support truthful people – the best examples of truthful people are prophets, because they bring truth from God.

## Guidance from the Quran and the Prophet's Best Example

وَمَن يُطِعِ اللَّهَ وَالرَّسُولَ فَأُولَٰئِكَ مَعَ الَّذِينَ أَنْعَمَ اللَّهُ عَلَيْهِم مِّنَ النَّبِيِّينَ وَالصِّدِّيقِينَ وَالشُّهَدَاءِ وَالصَّالِحِينَ وَحَسُنَ أُولَٰئِكَ رَفِيقًا

And whosoever obeys God and His messenger, such will be in the company of those whom God has blessed: the Prophets, the truthful ones, the martyrs, and the righteous. And how excellent a company of such people is. (Quran 4:69)

يَا أَيُّهَا الَّذِينَ آمَنُوا اتَّقُوا اللَّهَ وَقُولُوا قَوْلًا سَدِيدًا يُصْلِحْ لَكُمْ أَعْمَالَكُمْ وَيَغْفِرْ لَكُمْ ذُنُوبَكُمْ

Believers, fear Allah and say what is right; Allah will fix your affairs and forgive your sins. (Quran 33:70-71)

I order you to be truthful, for truthfulness leads to righteousness, and righteousness leads to Paradise. A man continues to be truthful and strives for truthfulness until he is written as a truthful person with God. And beware of falsehood, for indeed falsehood leads to sinning, and indeed sinning leads to the Fire. A man continues to tell lies and strives upon falsehood until he is written as a liar with God." (Hadith: Sahih Muslim)

## The effects of being truthful

- Truthfulness always leads to a good ending, even though it may hurt us at first.
- Being truthful keeps you away from unforeseen troubles.
- Trust is hard to gain, but once you are considered truthful, people start believing in you without asking.
- Truthfulness reassures our sense of accountability.
- It develops courage in us – speaking the truth to powerful people is not easy and requires moral courage and deep conviction.
- Truthfulness in business transactions brings blessings to God in this world and the Hereafter.
- When the Prophet's companions migrated to far lands after his death, millions of people accepted Islam because of their truthfulness and honesty in dealings.

## The end result is always good

### Example 1

When the Prophet told the people of Makkah about his vision of the night journey from Masjid al-Haram to Masjid al-Aqsa, Abu Bakr, his close friend, believed him immediately. The prophet nicknamed him "As Siddiq (the truthful one)" after that. He was also among the first ones to accept Islam. Allah honored him so greatly that he was always considered next to the Prophet in rank.

### Example 2

Ka'ab bin Malik and his two friends did not attend a battle with Prophet Muhammad without any legitimate reason. They thought about a lame excuse. However, when the Prophet asked him, he told the truth: he had not gone to the battle for worldly reasons, and he should have gone. People boycotted them for many days due to this behavior, but then Allah forgave them and mentioned them in the Quran, a big honor.

If truthfulness is a desirable attribute, why do so many people lie?

## Lying and its consequences

- Regardless of religion, no human being likes lying.
- Lying always leads to disastrous endings, even though it may gain us something briefly.
- Lying, if it becomes a habit, is the fountainhead of many vices and leads a person to wickedness.
- Lying shows a person's inner state and is a sign of a lack of true faith in God.
- The habit of lying in a society destroys society.
- The first impression is the last – you lose trust once because of lying, and it is hard to earn it again.
- One danger in lying is that we start taking it lightly – it is Satan's trap.

## Guidance from the life of Prophet Muhammad

A person lies and lies until he is written with God as a habitual liar. (Hadith: Sahih Al-Bukhari)

I guarantee a house in the middle of Paradise for the one who leaves off lying, even if it be in a joke. (Hadith: At-Tirmidhi)

The signs of a hypocrite are three (at the time of Prophet Muhammad): when he speaks, he lies; when he makes an oath, he breaks it; and when he is entrusted with something, he betrays that trust. (Hadith: Sahih Bukhari and Muslim)

The Prophet, at the age of 40, one day asked a large crowd of people from various tribes: "O People! Will you believe me if I tell you that your enemies intend to ambush you at dawn or night?" They answered, "We have not heard a lie from you throughout your life." At the age of 25, the Prophet already had earned the titles of al-Sadiq and al-Amin, "The Truthful and Trustworthy." (Seerah of the Prophet)

When, for the first time, the Prophet received divine revelation. He expressed his worry to his wife about this experience. While comforting him, she said: "By God! Allah will never humiliate you because you are always kind to your kin and are always truthful, and you bear the burden of others; you earn for the poor and are generous to guests and help those in distress. (Seerah of the Prophet)

A man came to Prophet Muhammad and said, "O Messenger of Allah, I have many bad habits. Which one of them should I give up first?" Prophet Muhammad said, "Give up telling lies first and always speak the truth." The man promised to do so and went home. Later, he decided to steal something that night but dropped the idea, thinking he would have to lie to the Prophet if the Prophet asked him about it. Similarly, one day, he decided to consume alcohol (which is prohibited in Islam), but thinking that he would have to lie in front of the Prophet if he asked him about alcohol, he did not. Slowly but gradually, he gave up all his bad habits after he stopped lying. (Seerah of the Prophet)

## Quick Recap

- Being truthful is the source of many righteous deeds – in other words, avoiding lying may stop you from committing bad deeds.
- Truthfulness is something that needs to be cultivated until it reflects in our character.
- Truthfulness is one of the manifestations of the consciousness of Allah.
- Truthfulness always leads to a good ending, even though it may hurt us at first.
- Being truthful keeps you away from unforeseen troubles.
- Lying, if it becomes a habit, is the fountainhead of many vices and leads a person to wickedness.
- The first impression is the last– you lose trust once because of lying, and it is hard to earn it again.

1. Are there situations when telling the truth may not be the right thing to do?
2. How does social media encourage us to spread lies?

# Chapter 12

# Honesty

This chapter covers the concept of honesty that we are all familiar with, but we take it lightly without realizing how dishonesty can destroy a society.

# Honesty is the best policy

- There is a famous proverb: "honesty is the best policy." This means that if there is one principle you want to adopt in your life, then that is honesty.

## Difference between truthfulness and honesty

| Truthfulness | Honesty |
|---|---|
| Expressing what you think is the fact and truth. | A moral quality that makes you refuse to lie, deceive, or cheat at any time. |

- The core idea of the relationship between the two is that truthfulness is the most effective and morally sound way to live in the long run. Being honest means being truthful.

## The concept of Honesty

- Honesty is sometimes closely related to truthfulness, but it is a wider quality than just being truthful – the virtue of honesty includes truthfulness in one's words, deeds, and intentions.
- Honesty is the fountainhead of many qualities, such as truthfulness, trustworthiness, patience, and contentment.
- Honesty is required in our dealings with God and our dealings with other human beings.
- For God, honesty is synonymous with sincerity.
- We should not just be honest and truthful, but also support and befriend honest and truthful people – sometimes, our company of friends shapes our character.
- We are usually not honest because we want to avoid getting into trouble, gain some temporary benefits, or make ourselves look better (cool).
- Adhering to a policy of honesty enables us to navigate challenges with both integrity and intelligence. By committing to the truth, we challenge ourselves to find creative solutions to difficult problems without ever compromising our values.

> Lying/cheating may be an easy way out, but honesty teaches us how to handle difficult situations in our lives.

## Honesty in actions and dealings

- What's important in being honest is that our outward actions must coincide with our inward state; the good words we say and the good deeds we do should be authentic expressions of the goodness in our hearts and our character, whether in public or private.
- There is great emphasis in Islam on dealing with people honestly – dishonesty often results in taking other people's rights, which makes it a sin.
- Like truthfulness, honesty should be practiced in every aspect, so it becomes our second nature, resulting in a pure heart.
- One aspect of honesty is fulfilling our obligations/promises to the best of our ability – when we fall short, we are not considered honest.
- When dealing with other people, we should remind ourselves that our actions and deeds are recorded by the two angels sitting on our right and left.
- Hurting others because of dishonesty requires us to ask not only for forgiveness from God but also from that person – it's a big deal.

## Trust and honesty

- When we are dishonest, we are breaking a trust that people have put in us that we will always be honest when dealing with them – that trust is like an unwritten contract between them and us.
- If we are not honest, we can never be trustworthy.
- When people ask for an honest opinion, they place trust in us, and we should give sincere advice.
- Some examples of where we break people's trust by being dishonest:
    - Buying and selling
    - Homework (think about how we can break the trust?)
    - Position of authority
    - Assignments/Exams
    - Contracts
    - Advice/Counsel

> The consulted one is in a position of trust. (Hadith, Al-Tirmidhi)

Which Prophet's nation was destroyed because of dishonesty, and what was their crime?

# Guidance from the Quran and Prophet Muhammad's Example

وَمَن يَغْلُلْ يَأْتِ بِمَا غَلَّ يَوْمَ الْقِيَامَةِ ۚ ثُمَّ تُوَفَّىٰ كُلُّ نَفْسٍ مَّا كَسَبَتْ وَهُمْ لَا يُظْلَمُونَ

Whosoever is dishonest in his trust, he will be presented with this dishonesty on the day of judgment, and he will be recompensed accordingly, and there will be no injustice. (Quran 3:161)

وَإِنَّ عَلَيْكُمْ    كِرَامًا كَاتِبِينَ    يَعْلَمُونَ مَا تَفْعَلُونَ

They do not realize that there are guardians appointed over them; they are honorable writers, and they know what you do. (Quran 82:10-12)

وَآتُوا الْيَتَامَىٰ أَمْوَالَهُمْ ۖ وَلَا تَتَبَدَّلُوا الْخَبِيثَ بِالطَّيِّبِ ۖ وَلَا تَأْكُلُوا أَمْوَالَهُمْ إِلَىٰ أَمْوَالِكُمْ ۚ إِنَّهُ كَانَ حُوبًا كَبِيرًا

"And give to the orphans their wealth/property, and do not substitute worthless (things) for (their) good (ones) and do not take their wealth (in addition to that) by mixing it with your wealth; this is surely a great sin." (Quran 4:2)

وَيْلٌ لِّلْمُطَفِّفِينَ    الَّذِينَ إِذَا اكْتَالُوا عَلَى النَّاسِ يَسْتَوْفُونَ وَإِذَا كَالُوهُمْ أَو وَّزَنُوهُمْ يُخْسِرُونَ

أَلَا يَظُنُّ أُولَٰئِكَ أَنَّهُم مَّبْعُوثُونَ    لِيَوْمٍ عَظِيمٍ    يَوْمَ يَقُومُ النَّاسُ لِرَبِّ الْعَالَمِينَ

"Woe to the cheaters (dishonest in measure); when they take from people, they take full, but when they give others, they cheat. Don't they think they will be resurrected on a great Day? On that day, people will be standing in front of the Lord of the Worlds.  (Quran 83: 1-6)

Aisha, the Prophet's wife, said, "There was no behavior more hateful to the Messenger of Allah than dishonesty. A man would tell a lie when speaking in the presence of the Prophet, and he would not be satisfied until he knew that he had repented." (Reported by Tirmidhi)

The Prophet passed by a pile of food and put his hand into it, and his fingers touched something wet. He said, "What is this, O seller of the food?" The man said, "It got rained on, O Messenger of Allah." He said, "Why did you not put it (the wet part) on top of the pile so that the people could see it? He who deceives does not belong to me." According to other reports, "He who deceives us is not one of us," or "He is not one of us who deceives us." (Hadith: Muslim)

Whenever a people cheat in weights and measures, provisions are cut off from them (or, in other words, the blessings in those provisions). (Hadith: Muwatta Imam Malik)

O people, if any of you is put in a position of authority on behalf of Muslims and then he conceals from us a needle or more, it would be considered dishonesty (in public funds), and he will have to produce it on the Day of Judgment". (Hadith: Muslim and Abu Dawud)

Whenever people cheat in weights and measures, they will be stricken with famine, severe calamity, and the oppression of their rulers. (Hadith: Ibn Majah)

## Effects of dishonesty in a society

- The people of Prophet Shuaib fell into ruin because they rejected the oneness of God and spread fraud and dishonesty in society.
- Honesty at the societal level is so important that it determines a nation's fate on the world stage.
- Short-changing people's due rights creates an atmosphere of mistrust and cheating within society, and that society is deprived of God's blessing.
- There is a surah in the Quran (can you tell which one?) that scolds people who cheat others in society when measuring out goods.
- Measuring perfectly can be applied to other areas, such as granting others rights. For example: returning something borrowed on time, an employee working 6 hours a day for the 8-hour pay they receive, a politician not addressing the issues they were elected to address.

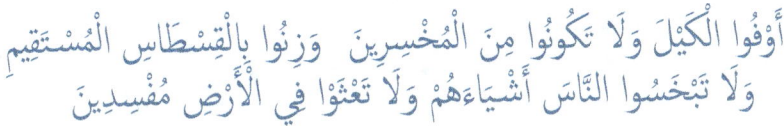

I tell you that you give the full measure, do not be among the cheaters, and weigh it with the correct balance. Do not give people less than they have bought, and do not spread corruption on earth. (Quran 26:181-183)

## Guidance from the life of Prophet Muhammad

In the Treaty of Hudaybiyah, Prophet Muhammad signed a contract with the non-Muslims of Makkah in which one of the unreasonable conditions was that if someone escaped Makkah and tried to join Prophet Muhammad in Medina during the period, Muslims would hand them over to non-Muslims unconditionally. This was not one of the conditions favoring Muslims, but Prophet Muhammad returned persecuted Muslims to non-Muslims at that time to abide by the contract. (Seerah)

Even when the Makkans persecuted Prophet Muhammad for the message of Islam, they still used to trust him with their belongings. When the Prophet decided to migrate to Medina due to persecution, he instructed his cousin Ali to stay behind in Mecca to return all the belongings the Prophet had from the people. (Seerah)

## Quick Recap

- The virtue of honesty includes truthfulness in one's words, deeds, and intentions.
- Lying/cheating may be an easy way out, but honesty teaches us how to handle difficult situations in our lives.
- When dealing with other people, we should remind ourselves that our actions and deeds are recorded by the two angels sitting on our right and left.
- Hurting others because of dishonesty requires us to ask not only for forgiveness from God but also from that person – it's a big deal.
- If we are not honest, we can never be trustworthy.
- Honesty at the societal level is so important that it determines a nation's fate on the world stage.
- Prophet Muhammad was the symbol of honesty in the society he lived in.
- Ironically, we don't want other people to cheat us, but we feel OK to cheat on other people.

**Golden Rule:** Do unto others as you would have them do unto you.

Can you be honest and wrong at the same time? Discuss some examples.

# Chapter 13

# Patience

This chapter covers the concept of patience, which is the most frequently mentioned attribute in the Quran, as it is a test for believers of God.

# The concept of Patience - صبر Sabr

- There is no single moral quality appreciated and promised paradise in the Quran more than PATIENCE.
- The word Sabr in Arabic means 'to hold back.' It means to endure something peacefully while trying to change the situation without letting it control our behavior.
- In the Quran and Islam, it now means 'to remain steadfast on a principle or course of action for a stand that you consider is right while seeking help from God.'
- Since this is a virtue, being steadfast on a wrong or immoral course is not considered patience.
- The next level of patience is 'beautiful patience' (**Sabrun Jameelun**), which means patience that displays the quality of excellence and kindness in response.
- In Islam, patience is required even when someone is given blessings to put

**Life = Test = Patience + Gratitude**

## Difference between patience and passiveness

Patience is developed over time.

Patience or *Sabr* is <u>not</u> a passive waiting.

- In the word Sabr, the concepts of patience and perseverance are combined. It may involve actively pursuing something without showing anxiety about the process and time it takes—sometimes referred to as 'active patience.'
- On the other hand, passiveness means 'wait' for something or doing nothing because of weakness and frailty, due to helplessness.
- Patience can be passive at times, depending on the situation, but the concept is usually associated with persevering toward a noble goal despite obstacles and setbacks.
- For example, if a subject is very difficult to study. Patience is involved here. Instead of constantly complaining about the subject, a believer should patiently accept the fact, understand what is lacking, and work hard to overcome the gaps and try to excel in that subject.
- The same applies to religious matters as well.

## Being patient is a trial from God

- As described in the chapter on gratitude, patience is another area where we are tested
- The reason Islam takes patience to the next level is that our attitude towards circumstances requiring patience has consequences in the Hereafter.
- One of God's practices in this world, when dealing with us, is that He has made this world a trial.
- The circumstances of sorrow and happiness, poverty and affluence, grief and joy that continuously befall people in this world are governed by this practice.
- When He afflicts someone with poverty, hardships, and other griefs, He tests whether that person will remain patient.
- We are required to be thankful for what we have, remain satisfied with our fate, and be honorable in our hardships or frustration, and let not disappointment end up in despair and dejection, show discontent with our fate, become angry with God, and live a life of misery in this world, and be questioned on the day of judgment for this behavior.
- If we attune our perspective on this life to this practice of God and remain mindful, it will help us lead a happy life with whatever we have and achieve success in the hereafter.

## Believer's most admirable quality

- Patience is the fountainhead of determination, resolve, and the pinnacle of human character that results in paradise in the Hereafter.
- No matter how difficult or easy the time is and whether we are patient and grateful or not, it will pass – it's our attitude that is tested during this time.
- If we accept that both times of ease and difficulty are from God, then it will help us through this with flying colors.
- All prophets were attributed with patience as their primary quality, which is required of them in their prophetic tasks.
- The believing patient is glorified in the Quran, so much so that when they enter into paradise, they will be told that they are there because of their faith and the patience they displayed.
- Patience is an admirable quality because it is not EASY to be patient.

**Two people, same situation, two results**

## Companions of patience

- As with many other attributes, patience goes hand in hand with other attributes and helps in their growth.

| | |
|---|---|
| **Patience and Gratefulness** | Gratitude is what is required. If we do not complain in addition to that and remain content with what we have, then it becomes patience. Both are good companions. |
| **Patience and Piety** | Piety here means being conscious of God when disobeying him or committing sin. Patience and piety help each other and stop us from disobeying God. |
| **Patience and Trust in God** | After making the desired efforts, we are required to hand the matter over to God for success. This requires patience, as results are in the hands of God alone. |
| **Patience and Forgiveness** | As we expect God to forgive us for our sins, we are encouraged to forgive others, which is not easy and requires a lot of patience. |
| **Patience and Sacrifice** | Ibrahim told Ismail about his dream in which he is shown sacrificing his son; Ismail answered that he will be patient. Sacrificing something for the sake of God requires patience. |
| **Patience and Wisdom** | The prophet and his companion were asked to return evil with goodness, and as a result, their fiercest enemies will become their friends. God said only patient people get this wisdom. |

## Patience is cultivated over time – A parable

- In order to understand how patience is cultivated over time, look at the example of a farmer growing a harvest.

Farmer ➡ tills the soil ✚ water ✚ constantly looks after ➡ Harvest

Believer ➡ tills the personality ✚ Faith ✚ carefully practices ➡ Patience

## Allah loves patience

وَلَئِنْ أَذَقْنَا الْإِنسَانَ مِنَّا رَحْمَةً ثُمَّ نَزَعْنَاهَا مِنْهُ إِنَّهُ لَيَئُوسٌ كَفُورٌ

وَلَئِنْ أَذَقْنَاهُ نَعْمَاءَ بَعْدَ ضَرَّاءَ مَسَّتْهُ لَيَقُولَنَّ ذَهَبَ السَّيِّئَاتُ عَنِّي ۚ إِنَّهُ لَفَرِحٌ فَخُورٌ

إِلَّا الَّذِينَ صَبَرُوا وَعَمِلُوا الصَّالِحَاتِ أُولَٰئِكَ لَهُم مَّغْفِرَةٌ وَأَجْرٌ كَبِيرٌ

If We Show Our mercy to man and deprive him of it, he becomes frustrated and ungrateful. And if after adversity We grant him favors, he says: "Gone are my hardships," and grows jubilant and boastful. But not the patient ones who do good deeds. Forgiveness is for them, and it is also a great reward. (Quran 11:9-11)

يَا بُنَيَّ أَقِمِ الصَّلَاةَ وَأْمُرْ بِالْمَعْرُوفِ وَانْهَ عَنِ الْمُنكَرِ وَاصْبِرْ عَلَىٰ مَا أَصَابَكَ ۖ إِنَّ ذَٰلِكَ مِنْ عَزْمِ الْأُمُورِ

O my son, establish prayers and enjoin virtue and forbid evil. Endure with patience any hardship that afflicts. No doubt, doing this is an act of determination. (Quran 31:17)

إِنَّمَا يُوَفَّى الصَّابِرُونَ أَجْرَهُم بِغَيْرِ حِسَابٍ

Indeed, the patient will be recompensed with no count. (Quran 39:10)

وَبَشِّرِ الصَّابِرِينَ الَّذِينَ إِذَا أَصَابَتْهُم مُّصِيبَةٌ قَالُوا إِنَّا لِلَّهِ وَإِنَّا إِلَيْهِ رَاجِعُونَ

أُولَٰئِكَ عَلَيْهِمْ صَلَوَاتٌ مِّن رَّبِّهِمْ وَرَحْمَةٌ ۖ وَأُولَٰئِكَ هُمُ الْمُهْتَدُونَ

And [O Prophet!] Give glad tidings to those who persevere [in their cause]. [Those] who, when afflicted with some calamity, say: "We belong to God, and to Him [one day] we shall return." On such people will be God's blessings and mercy, and it is they who will be rightly guided. (Quran 2:155-157)

What type of patience is required when Allah has given you a lot of blessings and happiness?

## Patience in our relationships

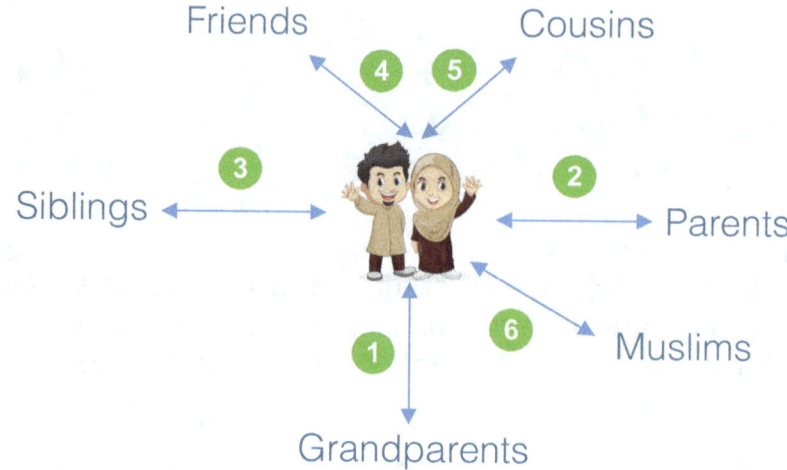

- If there is one place where we can cultivate it and develop it as part of our character, then that is our home. Most people miss this fact.
- Most people show patience everywhere except in their homes with their families and friends, and in the immediate environment they live in.
- Our test is around us, starting with the closest.
- Our grandparents need our patience the most because they sometimes ask for help more than anyone else.
- Our parents may ask us to do things we don't like.
- We also need to be patient with our younger siblings, as they may 'annoy' us, which we sometimes don't like.

## Occasions of patience

1. Loss of our loved ones.
2. Loss of health and facing short-term or long-term sickness, including terminal illness.
3. Insufficient provisions, including wealth, and unexpected hardship.
4. Wars and lack of peace.
5. People who maintain a bad attitude toward us and people who have harmed us.
6. Seeing wrong in society that you cannot do anything about.
7. When reconciling with people or when making a pact with someone.
8. When we see other people get something we cannot have but desire.

**Prophet's Golden Rule**   الصبر عند صدمة الاولى   Patience is most required when a calamity strikes.

## How to achieve patience?

The following things help in achieving patience

1. Strong faith in Allah SWT and His attributes of All-Knowing, All-Seeing, All-Wise, and Most-Just.
2. Trust in Allah, knowing that first, we must do our part; only then does help come from Allah SWT.
3. Always remember that this life is a test, and we are going through a trial in which our attitude is tested.
4. Sorrow and happiness, poverty and affluence, grief, and joy come in a cycle after each other.
5. Remember, difficulties and challenges come to raise you up and unleash your full potential.
6. Sickness and hardship remove minor sins from a Muslim.
7. Real life is the life in the Hereafter, and this life is temporary.
8. Tough times will come and go, regardless of your attitude – be smart.
9. We are asked to get assistance through prayer and patience.
10. Remember all the blessings that you have compared to the hardship you are facing.
11. Sharing it with close friends who are your well-wishers.
12. Paying attention to the people who are going through much more hardships than you.

## Guidance from the Quran

- Allah gave us the recipe for patience:

$$يَا أَيُّهَا الَّذِينَ آمَنُوا اسْتَعِينُوا بِالصَّبْرِ وَالصَّلَاةِ ۚ إِنَّ اللَّهَ مَعَ الصَّابِرِينَ$$

O Believers, seek help with patience, perseverance, and prayers. Indeed, Allah is with the people who persevere. (Quran 2:153)

- Angels on the day of judgment will welcome people saying:

$$سَلَامٌ عَلَيْكُم بِمَا صَبَرْتُمْ ۚ فَنِعْمَ عُقْبَى الدَّارِ$$

"Peace be upon you for what you patiently endured. And what an excellent final home this is." (13:24)

## Guidance from the Prophet's Best Example

The Prophet passed by a woman who was crying beside a grave. He told her to fear Allah and be patient. She said to him, "Go away, for you have not been afflicted with a calamity like mine." And she did not recognize him. Then, she was informed that he was the Prophet. So she went to the Prophet's house and said to him, "I did not recognize you." He said, "Verily, the patience is when the calamity first strikes." (Hadith: Sahih Bukhari, 23/372)

Excellent is the believer's affair, for there is good for him in every matter, and this is not the case with anyone except the believer. If he gets good, then he is grateful to Allah, and thus there is good for him, and if he is afflicted with harm, then he shows patience, and thus there is good for him.
(Hadith: Sahih Muslim 2999)

Some people from the Ansar asked the Prophet, and he gave them. Then they asked for more charity, and he gave them. Then they asked again, and he gave them until all he had was gone. The Prophet said, "If I had anything, I would not withhold it. Whoever refrains from asking others, then Allah will make him content. Whoever wants to be independent, then Allah will make them independent. Whoever is patient, then Allah will make him patient. No gift is better and more comprehensive than patience." (Hadith: Sahih Bukhari 6105, Sahih Muslim 1053)

If Allah intends good for someone, then He tests him with trials.
(Hadith: Sahih Bukhari 5321)

The Prophet's life is an excellent example for us to follow in patience. He was born an orphan, his mother passed away when he was 6, and he lost his grandfather when he was 9. During the social boycott, his wife and uncle died when he needed them most. He was forced into exile from his birthplace after facing the most brutal religious persecution from his family and tribe. He lost all his male children during his lifetime. (Seerah of the Prophet)

The Prophet was praying near the Ka'ba. A she-camel had just been slaughtered the day before. Abu Jahl, his arch-enemy, said, 'Who will go and bring the fetus of the she-camel and place it between the shoulders of Muhammad when he prostrates?' Uqbah ibn Abu Mu'ait got up, brought the fetus, and placed it between his shoulders when the Prophet went down to prostrate." They all laughed at him, and some nearly fell over with laughter. The Prophet had bent down his head in prostration and did not raise it until a man went to his house and informed his daughter, Fatima, a young girl (at that time). She came and removed (the filthy thing) from him. Then she turned towards them, rebuking them (Abu Jahl and his friends). When the Prophet ( peace be upon him) had finished his prayer, he made a dua to Allah SWT about this incident. (Seerah of the Prophet)

- There is no single moral quality appreciated and promised paradise in the Quran more than PATIENCE.
- The virtue of Sabr is comprehensive, encompassing many aspects of our lives.
- Patience is not passiveness and helplessness.
- This life is a test. The circumstances of sorrow and happiness, poverty and affluence, grief and joy that continuously befall people in this world are governed by this practice.
- The best way to be patient is to not take any blessing for granted and cherish what we have.
- If there is one place where we can cultivate the quality of patience and develop it as part of our character, then that is our home.
- We are asked to seek God's help with patience and prayers.
- Whenever the prophet faced hardship, he would pray two units of prayer and ask Allah for help.
- Pay attention to the people who are going through much more hardship than we are.

Compare a few examples of patience and passiveness.

Read the story of Prophet Yusuf in Surah Yusuf in the Quran and note down the events where the quality of patience was observed.

# Chapter 14

# Forgiveness

This chapter covers the concept of forgiveness. Allah loves repentance, and this is the only attribute that keeps us hopeful to earn the paradise of Allah.

# The concept of Forgiveness

We ask for forgiveness from God.

**God** ⟵

We forgive others and ask for their forgiveness.

⟷ **People**

- Forgiveness means to let go of other people's mistakes or harmful actions without feeling any resentment in our hearts.
- In Islam, it's a multi-dimensional virtue that is related to both God and humans.
- God is Most Merciful and Most Forgiving, and He asks us to do the same.
- Humans make mistakes – forgiveness is part of the process of correcting those mistakes.
- Intention plays a crucial role in forgiveness.
- Some mistakes are sins – be careful.
- Prophet Muhammad taught us beautiful duas to seek forgiveness from God.

> **To err is human, to forgive is <u>divine</u>.**

## How to repent?

- Repentance (Tauba) is a religious concept in which we 'fix' the wrong by going through a process.
- Repentance is related to sin only – do not plan your sins.
- God has made it mandatory upon Himself that if someone repents immediately after sinning, then He will forgive the person.
- The golden rule for acceptance of repentance – DO NOT DELAY.

إِنَّمَا التَّوْبَةُ عَلَى اللَّهِ لِلَّذِينَ يَعْمَلُونَ السُّوءَ بِجَهَالَةٍ ثُمَّ يَتُوبُونَ مِن قَرِيبٍ فَأُولَٰئِكَ يَتُوبُ اللَّهُ عَلَيْهِمْ ۗ وَكَانَ اللَّهُ عَلِيمًا حَكِيمًا
وَلَيْسَتِ التَّوْبَةُ لِلَّذِينَ يَعْمَلُونَ السَّيِّئَاتِ حَتَّىٰ إِذَا حَضَرَ أَحَدَهُمُ الْمَوْتُ قَالَ إِنِّي تُبْتُ الْآنَ وَلَا الَّذِينَ
يَمُوتُونَ وَهُمْ كُفَّارٌ ۚ أُولَٰئِكَ أَعْتَدْنَا لَهُمْ عَذَابًا أَلِيمًا

God's responsibility is to forgive only those who sin while overwhelmed with emotions and then **quickly** repent. It is they whom God forgives. God is all-knowing and wise. But He will not forgive those who sin all their lives and, when death comes to them, say: "Now I repent!" nor those who die as disbelievers. It is for these that We have prepared a grievous punishment. (Quran 4:17-18)

**Repentance** = Immediate + Remorse + Intention to not repeat + Ask for Forgiveness + Correct the wrong

## Prophet Adam and Satan

- The story of Prophet Adam and Satan in the Quran conveys a powerful message about the benefits of repentance and asking for forgiveness from Allah.
- Both Prophet Adam and Satan made a mistake and disobeyed Allah, but their different behavior resulted in different endings.
- Prophet Adam and his wife realized their mistake <u>immediately</u> and asked Allah for forgiveness. Allah not only forgave them but also taught them beautiful words for asking for forgiveness.
- We learned that dua from the Quran:

رَبَّنَا ظَلَمْنَآ اَنْفُسَنَا . وَ اِنْ لَّمْ تَغْفِرْ لَنَا وَ تَرْحَمْنَا لَنَكُوْنَنَّ مِنَ الْخٰسِرِيْنَ

Lord! We have been unjust to our souls. If you now do not forgive us and do not have mercy on us, we shall definitely be among the losers."

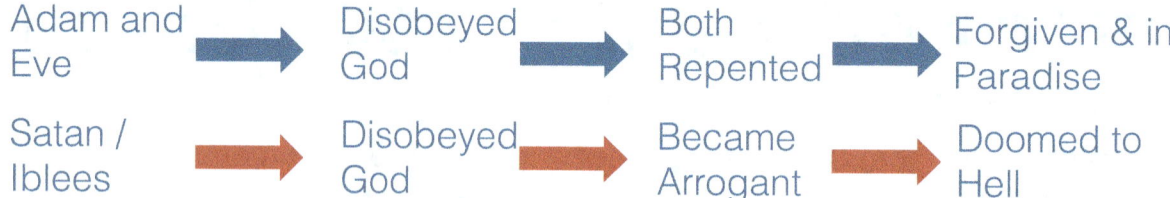

Be a son/daughter of Adam, not an agent of Satan

| Adam and Eve | → | Disobeyed God | → | Both Repented | → | Forgiven & in Paradise |

| Satan / Iblees | → | Disobeyed God | → | Became Arrogant | → | Doomed to Hell |

## Forgiveness in relationships

- If we expect God to forgive us for our mistakes, then we should forgive others for their mistakes – Forgive to be forgiven.
- Prophet Muhammad is the best example for us when it comes to forgiving others – learn his Seerah.
- Forgiving others is considered an essential attribute of believers in the Quran.
- Forgiving others is only related to the harm that affects you as a result.
- Forgiveness with wisdom and sincere advice is the best way to forgive.
- Studies in Psychology show that forgiving people are happier and healthier than unforgiving people – Try it.
- The best place to practice forgiveness is our home.

**Don't hold it! Let it go!**

# The companions of forgiveness

| | |
|---|---|
| **Forgiveness and Patience** | Forgiving others requires a big heart. It also requires a lot of patience. It is always good to practice patience and forgiveness together. |
| **Forgiveness and Courage** | Whether we are asking for forgiveness from others or forgiving them, both require courage to take the first step. |
| **Forgiveness and humility** | Humility is also one driving force for asking for forgiveness and forgiving others. Arrogance is the biggest hurdle to forgiveness. Satan is a good example. |
| Forgiveness and Anger Control | Controlling anger is also very helpful in forgiving others. Anger is usually the immediate reaction when someone harms us, and if we can let it subside quickly, we should be able to forgive |

## Forgiveness is not an excuse to sin

- Many of us do not take sin, repentance, and forgiveness seriously.
- We should not take Allah's Mercy and Forgiveness for granted and continue to repeat the same sin/mistake our entire life, thinking that we will ask for forgiveness one day.
- Remember, Allah knows what's in hearts and minds, and we cannot cheat Him.
- Some sins, when repeated, become major sins – e.g., small lies and cheating.
- Death is imminent, but we do not know its exact time; people repent immediately so as not to lose the chance.
- If Allah has guaranteed forgiveness immediately after the sin, then we should not wait.
- Just because we are not in 'trouble' even after committing sins or mistakes does not mean we will not be held accountable.
- Also, make it a practice to analyze your day when you go to bed and ask Allah for forgiveness for all your shortcomings during the day.

## Guidance from the Quran and Prophet's best examples

كَتَبَ رَبُّكُمْ عَلَى نَفْسِهِ الرَّحْمَةَ أَنَّهُ مَنْ عَمِلَ مِنكُمْ سُوءًا بِجَهَالَةٍ ثُمَّ تَابَ مِن بَعْدِهِ وَأَصْلَحَ فَأَنَّهُ غَفُورٌ رَّحِيمٌ

Your Lord has made Mercy compulsory upon Himself. And because of that, if any of you commits wrong out of ignorance or emotions and immediately repents after that and fixes what he has done wrong (with the intention not to commit it again), then Allah SWT is always Forgiving and always Merciful. (Quran 6:54)

قُلْ يَا عِبَادِيَ الَّذِينَ أَسْرَفُوا عَلَى أَنفُسِهِمْ لَا تَقْنَطُوا مِن رَّحْمَةِ اللَّهِ ۚ إِنَّ اللَّهَ يَغْفِرُ الذُّنُوبَ جَمِيعًا ۚ إِنَّهُ هُوَ الْغَفُورُ الرَّحِيمُ

Tell O Muhammad to those who have committed injustice to themselves by committing sins (even if it is Shirk), do not despair of the Mercy of Allah. Indeed, Allah forgives all sins. Indeed, He is Most Forgiving and always Merciful. (39:53)

الَّذِينَ يُنفِقُونَ فِي السَّرَّاءِ وَالضَّرَّاءِ وَالْكَاظِمِينَ الْغَيْظَ وَالْعَافِينَ عَنِ النَّاسِ ۗ وَاللَّهُ يُحِبُّ الْمُحْسِنِينَ

(Paradise is prepared for those) who spend their wealth in all conditions, whether ease or hardship, and they swallow their anger and forgive other people. Allah loves those who do good. (Quran 3:134)

Charity does not decrease wealth; no one forgives except that Allah increases his honor, and no one humbles himself for the sake of Allah except that Allah raises his status. (Hadith: Sahih Muslim 2588)

O Uqbah, reconcile whoever cuts you off, give to whoever deprives you, and pardon whoever wrongs you. (Hadith: Musnad Ahmad 16999)

I saw the Messenger of Allah, peace and blessings be upon him, tell the story of a prophet his people beat, and he wiped the blood from his face, saying: My Lord, forgive my people, for they do not know. (Hadith: Sahih Bukhari 6530)

Habbar ibn al-Aswad was a vicious enemy of Prophet Muhammad and Islam. He inflicted a severe injury on Zainab, the daughter of the Prophet, when she decided to migrate to Medina. She was pregnant when she started her migration, and the polytheists of Mecca tried to stop her from leaving. This man, Habbar bin al-Aswad, physically assaulted her and intentionally caused her to fall from her camel. Her fall had caused her miscarriage (death of the child), and she, herself, was severely hurt. He had committed many other crimes against Muslims as well. He wanted to flee to Persia, but when he decided to come to Prophet Muhammad instead, the Prophet magnanimously forgave him. **(Seerah of the Prophet)**

The tribe of Quraish was archenemies of Islam, and for a period of thirteen years, they would rebuke the Prophet, taunt and mock him, beat him, and abuse him, both physically and mentally. They plotted and attempted to kill him on more than one occasion, and when the Prophet migrated to Medina, they rallied most of the Arab tribes and waged many wars against him. Yet, when he entered Mecca victorious with an army of 10,000, he did not take revenge on anyone.

The Prophet said to the Quraish:

"O, people of Quraish! What do you think I will do to you? Hoping for a good response, they said: "You will do well. You are a noble brother, son of a noble brother." The Prophet said, "Then I say to you what Yusuf said to his brothers: 'There is no blame upon you today.' Go! You are all free!" Rarely in the annals of history can we read such an instance of forgiveness. Even his deadliest enemy, Abu Sufyan, who led so many battles against Islam, was forgiven, as was any person who stayed in his house and did not come to fight him. (Seerah of the Prophet)

## Guidance from the companions

The Prophet was sitting with a group of companions in the mosque. He suddenly said, "A man will now enter (who is) from the people of Paradise." The man walked in. Later, it happened again, and then a third time.

Abdullah ibn Amr ibn al-Aas wanted to find out what was so special about this individual, so he asked the man if he could stay at his house for three days, making an excuse to stay. The man allowed him to do so. After carefully observing him at home, Abdullah noticed that the man did nothing unusual. He didn't fast all the time; he slept some of the night, prayed some of the night, and so on. So, after three days, Abdullah told him the real reason he had asked him to stay with him, and he asked him what could be the reason he was from the people of Paradise. His host couldn't think of anything, but after some time, he said, "Every night, before I go to sleep, I forgive whoever has wronged me. I remove any ill feelings towards anyone from my heart and clean it." (Kitab al-Zuhd by Ibn Al-Mubarak, Number 694)

## Story of Abu Bakr (RA)

In Medina, the Prophet's wife, Aisha, was once slandered due to a false accusation against her. Aisha was innocent, but the slander spread within the community and caused a lot of grief to her, her father, Abu Bakr, and Prophet Muhammad. Abu Bakr was very upset about this incident. He used to financially support one family whose head was Mistah. When Abu Bakr learned that Mistah was also spreading rumors, he decided to stop financial support after Allah SWT declared Aisha innocent in the Quran.

At that moment, God reminded Abu Bakr of the noble attribute of forgiveness in the Quran:

وَلَا يَأْتَلِ أُولُو الْفَضْلِ مِنكُمْ وَالسَّعَةِ أَن يُؤْتُوا أُولِي الْقُرْبَىٰ وَالْمَسَاكِينَ وَالْمُهَاجِرِينَ فِي سَبِيلِ اللَّهِ ۖ وَلْيَعْفُوا وَلْيَصْفَحُوا ۗ أَلَا تُحِبُّونَ أَن يَغْفِرَ اللَّهُ لَكُمْ ۗ وَاللَّهُ غَفُورٌ رَّحِيمٌ

From among you, those who are affluent and whose provisions are extended (just because of this incident) should not vow that from now on, they will not be charitable to relatives, the needy, and those who immigrated for God. Let those people forgive them and let it go. Don't you want Allah to forgive you your sins? Indeed, Allah is Most Forgiving and Always Merciful (Quran 24:22)

Abu Bakr, after hearing this admonition, repented immediately. He forgave the man who slandered his daughter and continued to support him.

## Quick Recap

- God is Most Merciful and Most Forgiving, and He asks us to do the same.
- Humans make mistakes – forgiveness is part of the process of correcting those mistakes.
- Repentance = Immediate + Remorse + Intention to not repeat + Ask for Forgiveness + Correct the wrong.
- Both Adam and Satan disobeyed God, but Adam repented immediately.
- If we expect God to forgive us for our mistakes, then we should forgive others for their mistakes.
- Forgiveness requires patience, courage, humility, and self-control.
- We should not take Allah's Mercy and Forgiveness for granted and continue to repeat the same sin/mistake our entire life, thinking that we will ask for forgiveness one day.
- The best place to show forgiveness is with our family and friends.
- Let's learn some duas taught to us by Prophet Muhammad so we can make them part of our daily lives and ask for forgiveness.

Read the story of Prophet Yusuf in Surah Yusuf in the Quran and note the occasions where forgiveness is observed.

# Chapter 15

# Sympathy

This chapter covers the concept of sympathy. It's an attribute that Allah has bestowed in every human being, unless they have destroyed it.

# The concept of sympathy

- Sympathy is a natural feeling for other human beings that makes us sense their pain and suffering.
- Example: sharing your friend's feelings when his/her father died.
- Empathy is more intense when you put yourself in someone else's shoes.
- We are naturally more sympathetic towards our loved ones, including friends.
- Islam takes sympathy to another level as a virtue and wants us to help the person going through a difficult time.
- This natural urge exists because of this reason:

يَا أَيُّهَا النَّاسُ إِنَّا خَلَقْنَاكُم مِّن ذَكَرٍ وَأُنثَىٰ وَجَعَلْنَاكُمْ شُعُوبًا وَقَبَائِلَ

O people, We created you from a single pair of male and female and made you families and tribes, so you recognize each other. (Quran 49:13)

## Who needs our sympathy?

- Basically: **EVERYBODY!**
- As human beings, we should be sympathetic to every living being, including animals and plants.
- But naturally, our reactions, perspectives, and the extent of help and support may differ from person to person.
- People usually remember and appreciate more when we share their sorrow than their happiness!

## Brotherhood and sisterhood in Islam

- Brotherhood and sisterhood require compassion for each other.
- This relationship is beyond geographical borders.
- Action- not just words – cannot stand on the sidelines and feel sympathetic about people we can help.
- A requirement of our faith.
- Many of the world's sufferings are due to a lack of sympathy toward others.

> ### Believers are ONE
>
> إِنَّمَا الْمُؤْمِنُونَ إِخْوَةٌ
> Indeed, believers are brothers (and sisters) to each (Quran 49:10)
>
> ——— x ———
>
> "The parable of the believers in their affection, mercy, and sympathy for each other is that of a body. When any limb aches, the whole body reacts with sleeplessness and fever."
> (Hadith: Sahih Bukhari 5665)

## Examples of Sympathy – family of deceased

- Sending a message of condolence and asking if they need help.
- Visiting them when it is convenient for them.
- Listen to their grief and, if necessary, give them sincere advice.
- Work within your circle and plan how you can all help.
- Provide financial support to someone who has lost his/her breadwinner.
- Stay in touch with them for the next few days and weeks.
- Prepare some food and share it with them when visiting them.
- Don't be an intruder but a sincere helper/supporter.
- Take care of their young children, if any.
- Don't share the news until they ask you to.
- Make dua for them and their loved ones.

Imagine your city has recently received refugees from a war-torn country. Discuss how you would sympathize with them.

## Guidance from Prophet's Best Example

"Whoever relieves the hardship of a believer in this world, Allah will relieve his hardship on the Day of Resurrection. Whoever helps ease one in difficulty, Allah will make it easy for him in this world and the Hereafter. Whoever conceals the faults of a Muslim, Allah will conceal his faults in this world and the Hereafter. Allah helps the servant as long as he helps his brother. (Hadith: Sahih Muslim)

The Prophet said: 'I start praying, and I want to make it long, but then I hear an infant crying, so I make my prayer short because I know the distress caused to the mother by his crying.' (Hadith: Ibn Majah)

Prophet Muhammad was sitting with his companions when a funeral procession passed them, so he stood up. The companions said, 'O Prophet of Allah, it is the funeral procession of a Jew.' He said: 'Is it not a human soul?' (Hadith: Al-Bukhari and Muslim)

## Quick Recap

- Sympathy is a natural feeling for other human beings that makes us sense their pain and suffering.
- Islam takes sympathy to another level as a virtue and wants us to help those struggling.
- Many sufferings around us and in the world are due to the lack of sympathy toward others.
- We can do many things to help – if there is a will, there is a way.
- It creates a bond of mutual love. People remember and appreciate more when we share their sorrow than their happiness!

Should we sympathize with a murderer? Why and how?

# Chapter 16

# Selflessness

This chapter covers the concept of selflessness, which is a difficult attribute to understand. Let explore it and how to create a balance in your life when it comes to selflessness.

# The concept of selflessness

Every creation of God is **Selfless**

Be like them!

- People who think more about others and less about themselves, especially in times of need.
- Giving preference to others over oneself despite the need.
- Selfishness is one of the strongest urges in human beings.
- One of the most forgotten morals of Islam.
- Hard to find selfless people – if you know one, treasure them.
- It's the fruit of many virtues like humility, sympathy, gratitude, mercy, and generosity.
- This quality is needed in difficult times, such as the COVID-19 pandemic.

**You can be selfish for your success in the hereafter by being selfless in this life.**

## Selflessness in Islam

- It is also called "**Al-eeth'ar**," which means "sacrifice" or "altruism."
- It builds the bond that every family and community needs.
- The companions of Prophet Muhammad are a great example for us.
- The establishment of the 'Madinan brotherhood' after migration displayed the best acts of selflessness.
- The Quran commended their selflessness.

## Quiz – Who is this person?

✓ This person is a symbol of selflessness.
✓ The most loving person in the world.
✓ Always willing to sacrifice everything for you.
✓ Everyone has one.

# Guidance from the Quran

لَن تَنَالُوا الْبِرَّ حَتَّىٰ تُنفِقُوا مِمَّا تُحِبُّونَ

You can never attain piety until you spend from what you love. (Quran 3:92)

وَيُطْعِمُونَ الطَّعَامَ عَلَىٰ حُبِّهِ مِسْكِينًا وَيَتِيمًا وَأَسِيرًا إِنَّمَا نُطْعِمُكُمْ لِوَجْهِ اللَّهِ لَا نُرِيدُ مِنكُمْ جَزَاءً وَلَا شُكُورًا

And they feed the poor, orphans, and prisoners even when they need it most, with the passion that 'we only feed you to earn the pleasure of Allah and we do not seek any reward from you or any thanks'. (Quran 76:8-9)

يُحِبُّونَ مَنْ هَاجَرَ إِلَيْهِمْ وَلَا يَجِدُونَ فِي صُدُورِهِمْ حَاجَةً مِّمَّا أُوتُوا وَيُؤْثِرُونَ عَلَىٰ أَنفُسِهِمْ وَلَوْ كَانَ بِهِمْ خَصَاصَةٌ ۚ وَمَن يُوقَ شُحَّ نَفْسِهِ فَأُولَٰئِكَ هُمُ الْمُفْلِحُونَ

(These Ansar) love their brothers who have migrated to their land, and they do not feel any apprehension towards what's been given to them, and they prefer them over themselves even when they are in need. Indeed, whoever has been saved from selfishness will find true success in the hereafter. (Quran 59:9)

## Golden Rules

None of you is a believer until he loves for his brother that which he loves for himself." (Hadith –Bukhari & Muslim)

## Balancing between self and selflessness

- It is said that the best charity is given in times of difficulty or calamity.
- For example, it is nice to be charitable every day and take care of others, but when a calamity or disaster hits, then being charitable is not an option but mandatory.
- Also, you have to strike a balance among your needs, your family's needs, and society's needs.

**PREFERENCE IN TIMES OF NEED**

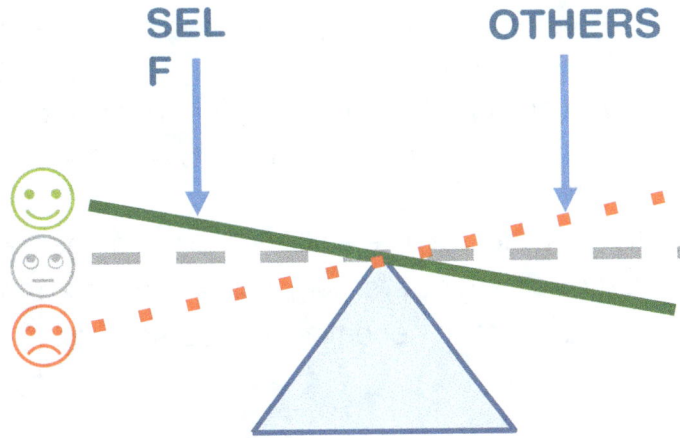

- In general, Islam is a religion of moderation and demands balance.
- In certain circumstances, we are required to temporarily abandon this balance.
- Maintain your position of 'giving' by taking care of yourself and your loved ones.
- Also, your body and the self have a right to yourself.
- Avoiding selfishness can lead to selfless acts.

## Guidance from the Prophet's Examples

A man once came to the Prophet Muhammad seeking food. The Prophet asked one of his wives for assistance, but she replied that she had only water. Then he sent the same message to another wife and received the same reply.

The Prophet said, "Who will entertain this man as a guest tonight?"
One of the Ansar said, "O Messenger of Allah, I will."

So the Ansari asked his wife to prepare food for the man, but she replied that they only had enough food to feed the children. With the intent to receive the reward from Allah, the man told his wife to keep the children busy and put them to bed when they asked for food.

When the guest entered, the host extinguished the light and made it appear as if they were eating. But they spent the night hungry so their guest could eat.

The next morning, the Prophet saw the Ansari man and informed him that Allah was pleased with his selflessness. **(Bukhari and Muslim)**

## How to be selfless

- Rule #: Don't be selfish.
- Share instead of 'take all' or 'give all'.
- If a matter affects a large number of people, prioritize the benefits that matter most.
- If you don't prefer something for yourself, don't prefer it for others.
- Only in unusual circumstances break the balance while maintaining your position of 'giving'.
- If everyone is a little selfless, we will all be happy – reciprocate.
- 'Buy' hereafter by 'selling' some of your world – it's a trade.
- Practice until it becomes your personality.

## Quick Recap

- Selfishness is one of the strongest urges in human beings.
- We should fight with ourselves and become a little more selfless.
- It's the fruit of many virtues like humility, sympathy, gratitude, mercy, and generosity.
- It builds the bond that every family and community needs.
- In general, Islam is a religion of moderation and demands balance.
- Unusual times seek sacrifices.
- The establishment of the 'Madinan brotherhood' after migration displayed the best acts of selflessness.
- If everyone is a little selfless, we will all be happy – reciprocate.

Discuss three examples in life when you should be:
a) The balanced/moderate selfless
b) Completely selfless
c) Selfish

Pick two creations of Allah and tell us how they are selfless by their nature.

# Chapter 17

# Kindness

This chapter covers the concept of kindness, which is quite widely known, but in Islam, it has taken it to the next level.

# The concept of Kindness

**Little drops of water make the mighty ocean**

- Kindness is at the core of many virtues – selflessness, mercy, and generosity.
- It's a general quality of being pleasant, generous, and considerate.
- Like other qualities, it's a requirement of our faith.
- Generosity, charity, and altruism must accompany kindness.
- Kindness is contagious.
- Do not undervalue small acts of kindness.

Every act of kindness is a charity. (Hadith: Bukhari, Muslim)

## Kindness in relationships

- In human relationships, we are asked to show 'Ehsan,' an excellent form of kindness.
- Kindness can be displayed through gentleness, leniency, compassion, and generosity.
- It is required in speech and action.
- It can turn the tide.
- God asked Musa to deal with Pharaoh (who raised him) with kindness so that he might change his behavior.
- Prophet Muhammad was the most kind to his companions and the people around him.

There has certainly come to you a Messenger from among yourselves. Grievousness to him is what you suffer from, for he is concerned over your matters, and to the believers, he is kind and merciful. (Quran 9:128)

## Kindness to our parents

- Most forgotten virtue in modern societies.
- Kindness to parents is a gateway to Paradise.
- The Quran combines worship of God and kindness to parents in many places.
- They were kind and will always be kind to you.
- We are warned against being disrespectful and unkind to parents.
- When they get old, we have to deal with them more than just with kindness.
- Disagree with your parents while being KIND.
- Always make dua for them.

وَبِالْوَالِدَيْنِ إِحْسَانًا

Treat your parents with (excellent form of) KINDNESS

It's sad if we are kind to our friends but not to our PARENTS. ☹

### Kindness 'Package' for Parents

✓ Mercy
✓ Compassion
✓ Respect
✓ Patience
✓ Generosity

## Guidance from the Quran and the Prophet's Best Example

قَوْلٌ مَّعْرُوفٌ وَمَغْفِرَةٌ خَيْرٌ مِّن صَدَقَةٍ يَتْبَعُهَا أَذًى

A kind word and act of overlooking is better than the charity that follows maltreatment. (Quran 2:263)

وَلَا تَسْتَوِي الْحَسَنَةُ وَلَا السَّيِّئَةُ ۚ ادْفَعْ بِالَّتِي هِيَ أَحْسَنُ فَإِذَا الَّذِي بَيْنَكَ وَبَيْنَهُ عَدَاوَةٌ كَأَنَّهُ وَلِيٌّ حَمِيمٌ

Good and evil are not the same; repel evil with what is better in conduct (goodness), and you will see that the person who has enmity with you will become like a close friend. (Quran 41:34)

"If Allah SWT intends goodness for a household, He lets kindness come over them." (Hadith: Masnad Ahmad 23906)

"O Aisha, Allah is kind and loves kindness in all matters." (Hadith: Sahih Bukhari 6528)

A man came to the Prophet asking, 'Who among the people is the most worthy of my good companionship (kindness)? The Prophet said, Your mother. The man said, 'Then who?' The Prophet said, then your mother. The man further asked, 'Then who?' The Prophet said, then your mother. The man asked again, 'Then who?' The Prophet replied, then your father. (Hadith: Sahih Al-Bukhari, Sahih Muslim)

## Kindness to animals

- Show kindness to everything that is 'living'.
- Abusing animals or other creatures of God will have consequences in the hereafter.
- The Quran mentions that all creatures on earth praise God in their way (24:41).

- We are made the custodians of this earth, and we should be gentle towards every creature that shares it.
- Every creature on earth serves a purpose.
- Islam prohibits killing animals for sport.
- In general, Muslim societies are not kind to animals.

There is a reward for kindness to every living thing. (Hadith: Bukhari)

وَمَا مِن دَابَّةٍ فِي الْأَرْضِ وَلَا طَائِرٍ يَطِيرُ بِجَنَاحَيْهِ إِلَّا أُمَمٌ أَمْثَالُكُم

Whichever creature walks on earth and birds fly in the skies, they are all communities like you. (Quran 6:38)

## From the life of Prophet Muhammad

One morning, a poor person brought fresh fruit from his small farm for Prophet Muhammad. People in those days used to do that for their love of Prophet Muhammad.

The Prophet accepted the gift, tasted it, and then continued eating it alone while the companions sat beside him, watching him eat the fruit. This had never happened before, as the Prophet had always shared the food with his companions.

One of the companions gently asked, "O Messenger of Allah, have you overlooked the right of those who watched while you ate it?"

Prophet Muhammad smiled and waited till the poor man who had brought the fruit had gone. Then he said, "I tasted the fruit, and it was not ripe yet. If I had given some of it to you, one of you would find it tasteless and say it tastes bad. That would have disappointed the poor man. So I decided to eat the whole fruit myself.

A group of companions once traveled with the Prophet Muhammad. During the journey, he went somewhere alone and left them for a while. During his absence, they saw a bird with its two young and took the young from the nest. The mother bird circled in the air, beating its wings in grief. When the Prophet came back and saw this, he asked, "Who has hurt the feelings of this bird by taking its young? Return them to her immediately." (Hadith: Muslim)

Once, Asma bint Abu Bakr's mother, who was still an unbeliever, came to see her in Madinah. She told the Prophet this: "My mother has come to see me and is expecting something from me. May I oblige her?" The Prophet said: "Yes, be kind to your mother" (Hadith: Muslim, 2195)

## From the life of companions

On the road to Mecca, Abdullah Bin Omar once met a Bedouin. He greeted him with peace, had him ride the mount he was riding, and gave him the turban he had been wearing. One of Abdullah's companions commented, "May God guide you; they are just Bedouin, and they are content with something simple." Abdullah answered, "The father of this man was a close friend of my father, and I heard the Prophet Muhammad say, "The best way of honoring one's parents is for the children to honor their father's friends." (Lives of companions)

## (Not so) Small acts of kindness

- Sometimes we are deceived into thinking we should do something big to help people or earn the pleasure of Allah. We should not wait for those moments but rather pay attention to what small things we can do every day.

- If someone owes you something, be easy or forgive.
- Teach someone a good piece of knowledge.
- Plant a tree.
- Get someone a bottle of water.
- Reconcile between two people.
- Help your parents with chores and/or groceries.
- Remove debris or something harmful from the path.
- Write a review for a business that has done a good job.
- Smile.
- Change the subject during a heated debate.
- Give up your seat for someone.
- Take care of little siblings while mom is cooking.
- Take the trash can out or put it back.
- Give up your position in the queue if someone is in need.

## Quick Recap

- It's a general quality of being pleasant, generous, and considerate.
- Do not undervalue small acts of kindness.
- Every act of kindness is a charity.
- Kindness can be displayed through gentleness, leniency, compassion, and generosity.
- It is required in speech and action.
- It can turn the tide.
- Kindness to parents is a gateway to Paradise.
- Show kindness to everything that is 'living'.
- No act of kindness is small.

Plan three small acts of kindness that you will do regularly from now on. Please share it with others next week for encouragement.

# Chapter 18

# Generosity

This chapter covers the concept of generosity in Islam, which is slightly different than charity but related.

# The concept of Generosity

## Charity and Generosity

- Sometimes, the concepts of charity and generosity are mixed and are considered the same, but there are a few differences.
- It is quite possible that a person may be very generous but not charitable, and vice versa.
- In Islam, a charitable person should be generous, and vice versa; thus, they are considered the same attribute.
- However, there may be people who could show these two behaviors, which are not appreciated in Islam:
    1. A person spends money on their relatives, children, friends, and society in general and is very generous, but does not pay attention to the poor or the needy. That person is definitely generous but not charitable at all.
    2. Similarly, a person might be taking care of the needs of poor people but becomes very stingy when it comes to spending on their children, family, and friends. That person is charitable but shows limited generosity.
- In Islam, we are asked to be moderate in everything. As we care for society and the needy, we should also take care of our family and friends.
- The **golden rule** is: Whatever we spend on our family, relatives, friends, and society is a charity if done for the sake of Allah.

| Charity | Generosity |
|---|---|
| - The most cherished virtue.<br>- Spending money on those who are poor and need financial help.<br>- One portion of charity is obligatory.<br>- A charitable person may or may not be generous.<br>- Islam extends charity beyond money.<br>- We should be charitable. | - The most cherished virtue.<br>- Spending money in your surroundings, including people, regardless of their financial status.<br>- Done completely voluntarily.<br>- A generous person may or may not be charitable.<br>- Generosity is mostly restricted to money, but can also be general.<br>- We should be generous. |

"For where your treasure is, there your heart will also be."
(attributed to Jesus)

# Charity/Generosity in Islam

- Let's look at what Allah wants from a believer:

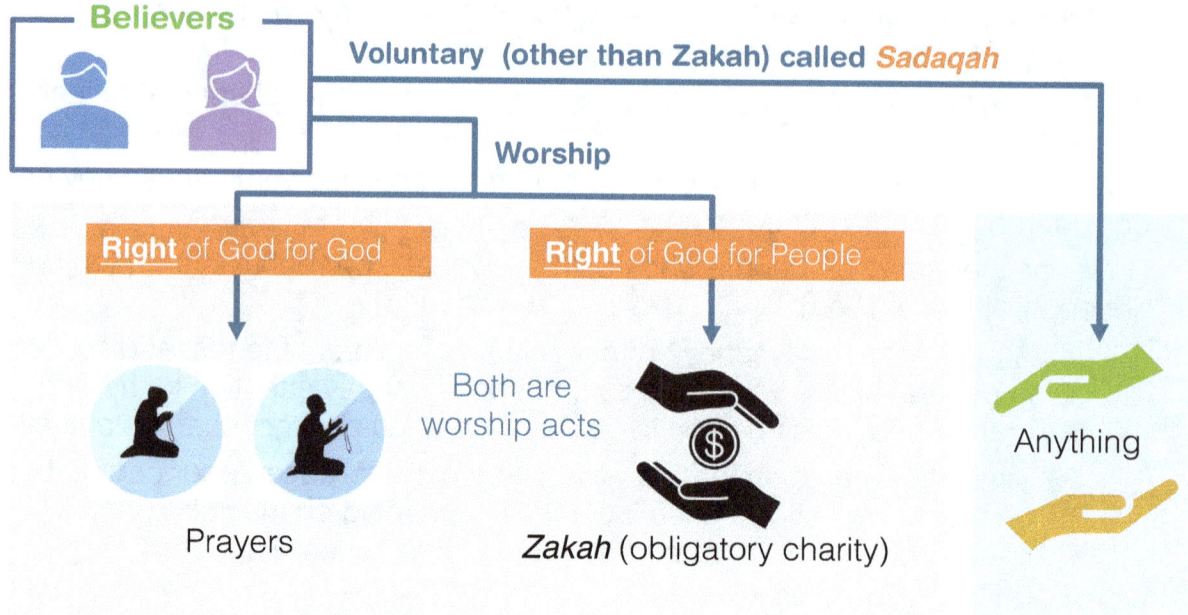

- It is a human tendency to help when they see people in need. However, Islam turned this natural human inclination into a form of worship and made it mandatory for Muslims to spend money on needy people and other charitable works.

- That fixed and mandatory portion is called Zakat.

- The purpose of Zakat in Islam is wider than just helping the poor.

- In Islam, Zakah is collected by the government to run its affairs, including helping people. It's a type of tax a government imposes on its citizens, but in this case, the rate of Zakat is fixed by Allah.

- Whatever we spend on top of Zakah is called *Sadaqah* (although Zakah is also Sadaqah, but it's a mandatory Sadaqah).

- So, for example, if you have $100 and are eligible to pay Zakah, you will pay, for example, $2.5 to the government for Zakah. Any amount you spend after that on any charitable work in the year is considered Sadaqah from you.

- Allah encourages voluntary Sadaqah in the Quran.

The upper hand is better than the lower hand.
(Hadith)

# The guidance from the Quran

لَيْسَ الْبِرَّ أَن تُوَلُّوا وُجُوهَكُمْ قِبَلَ الْمَشْرِقِ وَالْمَغْرِبِ وَلَٰكِنَّ الْبِرَّ مَنْ آمَنَ بِاللَّهِ وَالْيَوْمِ الْآخِرِ وَالْمَلَائِكَةِ وَالْكِتَابِ وَالنَّبِيِّينَ وَآتَى الْمَالَ عَلَىٰ حُبِّهِ ذَوِي الْقُرْبَىٰ وَالْيَتَامَىٰ وَالْمَسَاكِينَ وَابْنَ السَّبِيلِ وَالسَّائِلِينَ وَفِي الرِّقَابِ وَأَقَامَ الصَّلَاةَ وَآتَى الزَّكَاةَ وَالْمُوفُونَ بِعَهْدِهِمْ إِذَا عَاهَدُوا ۖ وَالصَّابِرِينَ فِي الْبَأْسَاءِ وَالضَّرَّاءِ وَحِينَ الْبَأْسِ ۗ أُولَٰئِكَ الَّذِينَ صَدَقُوا ۖ وَأُولَٰئِكَ هُمُ الْمُتَّقُونَ

The righteousness is not that you turn your face towards the East or the West. But the truly righteous is the one who believes in Allah and the day of Judgment, the angels, the books, the prophets, and who spends their wealth, despite their need for it, on their relatives, the orphans, the poor, the way fairer, on those who ask, and on freeing slaves while they establish prayers, pay their Zakah and fulfill their contracts once they agree. And they are patient in times of difficulty, illness, and times of war. These are the people who are truthful to God, and they are the ones who are God-conscious. (Quran 2:177)

إِن تُبْدُوا الصَّدَقَاتِ فَنِعِمَّا هِيَ ۖ وَإِن تُخْفُوهَا وَتُؤْتُوهَا الْفُقَرَاءَ فَهُوَ خَيْرٌ لَّكُمْ ۚ وَيُكَفِّرُ عَنكُم مِّن سَيِّئَاتِكُمْ ۗ وَاللَّهُ بِمَا تَعْمَلُونَ خَبِيرٌ

If you give your charity openly, then it is also fine, but if you give it in secret to help the poor, then it is better for you. God will reward you for this and remove your sins, and indeed, Allah knows what you do. (Quran 2:271)

 Quran shifted the whole paradigm of ownership and possessions.

- All blessings, including money, are given to us by God. When you give, you actually share what you have been given by God. Whatever extra that Allah gave you beyond your needs is for others, starting from your nearest ones.
- However, adopt a middle way when spending on charity.
- Be charitable all the time (not just in Ramadan).
- Give secretly and openly.
- Charity starts with your closest ones.
- Charity multiplies our blessings.
- Prayers and charity come together in many verses as signs of true believers.
- The word "spending" is mentioned hundreds of times in the Quran.
- Holding charity in times of need when you can afford it has severe consequences in the hereafter.

## Levels of faith

- Spending money on others is not easy. It tests our faith in Allah.
- However, the faith demands our behavior in accordance with the circumstances.
- Sometimes, we have to go beyond our regular spending to help out others.

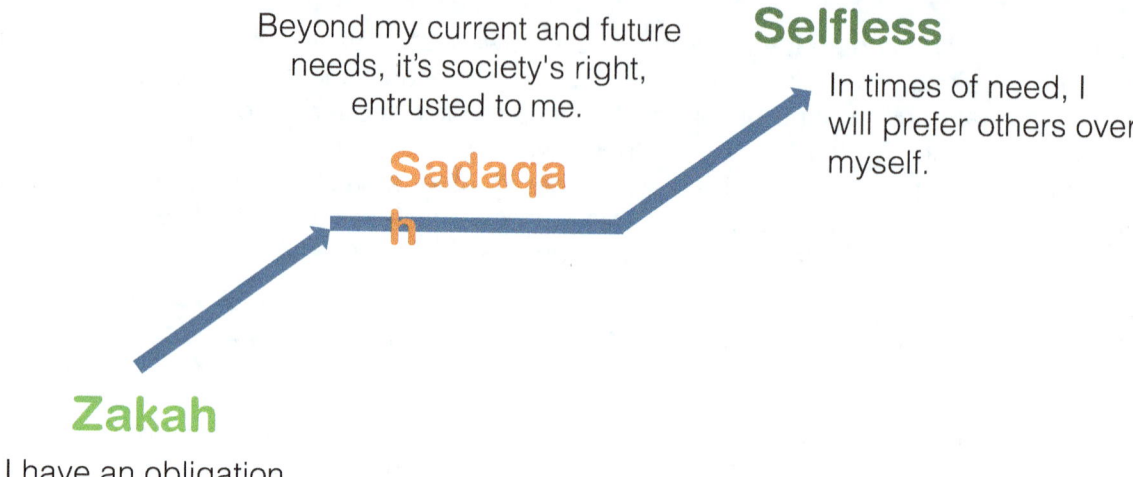

Beyond my current and future needs, it's society's right, entrusted to me.

**Sadaqah**

**Selfless**

In times of need, I will prefer others over myself.

**Zakah**

I have an obligation to fulfill.

مَّثَلُ الَّذِينَ يُنفِقُونَ أَمْوَالَهُمْ فِي سَبِيلِ اللَّهِ كَمَثَلِ حَبَّةٍ أَنبَتَتْ سَبْعَ سَنَابِلَ فِي كُلِّ سُنبُلَةٍ مِّائَةُ حَبَّةٍ ۗ وَاللَّهُ يُضَاعِفُ لِمَن يَشَاءُ ۚ وَاللَّهُ وَاسِعٌ عَلِيمٌ

The parable of those who spend their property in the way of Allah is as the parable of a grain growing seven ears (with) a hundred grains in every ear; and Allah multiplies for whom He pleases; and Allah is Ample-giving, Knowing. (Quran 2:261)

وَأَنفِقُوا مِن مَّا رَزَقْنَاكُم مِّن قَبْلِ أَن يَأْتِيَ أَحَدَكُمُ الْمَوْتُ فَيَقُولَ رَبِّ لَوْلَا أَخَّرْتَنِي إِلَىٰ أَجَلٍ قَرِيبٍ فَأَصَّدَّقَ وَأَكُن مِّنَ الصَّالِحِينَ

And spend from what we have given you before one of you reaches his/her death and regretfully says that O Lord, why didn't you give me more time in the world so that I would spend in your path, and I would become among the righteous. (Quran 63:10)

If our spending on others determines our faith, then why are some philanthropists (donors) individuals who do not believe in any God?

## Charity around you

- God wants people to take care of their:
  - Immediate family
  - Extended family
  - Friends
  - Neighbors
  - People whom we know
  - Community

- The order above must be maintained.
- Our generosity or charity MUST start from home and go outward. It makes no sense that we help people in other countries or spend money on charities like building mosques, but we have people in our immediate and extended family who go without food or the basic needs of life, like shelter.
- Remember, we will be **asked** about our family, relatives, and people around us.
- Also, what is considered a basic necessity today may be very different from the past. For example, today, education is considered a basic necessity.
- Also, money is just one form of charity. We can be charitable with our time, care, attention, etc.
- Charity should be given regardless of religion and race.
- One of the best ways to be 'charitable' in the society that we live in is to give some of our time to noble causes.
- One of the trials of gratitude is sharing the blessings with others.

## Generosity

- Although we looked at charity as a form of generosity, let's understand generosity separately.
- Generosity is a virtue not tied to the poor only, but to everything around us. It is an attitude of giving freely without expecting a return.
- We should be generous with our time, money, personal attention, care, kindness, etc. But generosity does NOT mean being wasteful or giving so much that we are left with nothing.
- Islam is a religion of moderation, and we are asked to be moderate in spending and act wisely.
- We see the general atmosphere of generosity during Ramadan. When inviting people to our houses or visiting others', we should be generous within our means.
- Being generous brings happiness, contentment, and blessings into our lives. We should be generous only for good causes.

## A story from the Quran – People of the Garden (Surah Al-Qalam)

- The Quran mentioned the story of the garden owners tested for charity.
- They vowed that they would pick all the fruits (harvest) and they would not leave anything on the trees for the poor and the needy.
- Knowing their intention, God destroyed their garden through high winds, and it seemed as if it had already been harvested while they were asleep.
- In the morning, they set out saying, 'Today, no beggar should be allowed to enter the garden to reach you'.
- They could not believe it when they reached there, thinking they had lost their way.
- The best one among them said, 'Did I not keep telling you to glorify God and be grateful to Him?' (Meaning, being charitable is one way to be grateful for the blessings one has.).
- They turned toward their Lord, repenting for their behavior.

## Guidance from Prophet's Best Example

Charity is obligatory every day on every joint of a human being. Your smiling at your brother's face is charity. Advising good and forbidding evil is charity. If one helps a person ride on his animal or lift his luggage onto it, all this will be regarded as charity. A good word, and every step one takes to offer the compulsory congregational prayer, is regarded as charity; guiding somebody on the road is regarded as charity, and removing harm from the road is a charity. (Hadith: Sahih Al-Bukhari)

When a man dies, his deeds come to an end except for three things: Continuous charity, knowledge left behind that is beneficial, or a virtuous child who prays for the deceased. (Hadith: Sahih Muslim)

Protect yourself from hellfire even by giving a piece of date as charity. (Hadith: Sahih Al-Bukhari and Muslim)

Allah, the Exalted, says, 'Spend, O son of Adam, and I shall spend on you.' (Hadith: Al-Bukhari and Muslim)

Charity does not in any way decrease the wealth. (Hadith: Sahih Muslim)

One day, Prophet Muhammad offered prayer in the mosque, hurried home, and returned immediately. A companion asked why he left, and he replied, "I left a piece of gold at home which was given for charity, and I disliked letting it remain at night in my house, so I brought it to the mosque to distribute." (Hadith: Sahih Al-Bukhari)

One day, Prophet Muhammad slaughtered a sheep in the house. Before leaving the house, he asked his wife, Aisha, to distribute the meat among the neighbors and the poor people. When he returned, he asked Aisha if she had distributed the meat of the sheep they had slaughtered. She told him: 'Nothing is saved but the shoulder,' knowing that Prophet Muhammad likes the shoulder of the sheep. He said, "Actually, everything except the shoulder is saved." (Seerah of Prophet Muhammad)

> Whatever we give to other people for the sake of God is saved by God and multiplied.

## Quick Recap

- Being generous and charitable are two virtues we should aim for, as these are among the most admired virtues in the Quran.
- One form of charity is Zakah, which is obligatory and is part of worship. The other form is voluntary and is called Sadaqah.
- Prayers and charity are often mentioned together in many verses as signs of true believers.
- The upper hand is better than the lower hand.  Give in secret and openly.
- Charity starts with your closest ones.
- Adopt a middle way when spending on charity.
- We should be generous with our time, money, personal attention, care, kindness, etc.
- Starting from Zakah, we should be charitable and, in difficult times, selfless.

# Remember,
# All blessings belong to God

You can be charitable without money. Identify a few acts of charity and generosity that you would regularly do from now on.

# Chapter 19

# Modesty

This chapter covers the concept of generosity in Islam. Human beings are born modest, but over time, people have adopted different ways. Let's learn what Islam has to say about modesty, as it covers more than just how to dress.

# The concept of Modesty  حياء

- There is no single English word that captures the true concept of Haya.
- **Haya** combines modesty and chastity and encompasses many other aspects of our personality.
- Required from both men and women.
- More than just how to dress and act in front of the opposite gender.
- It has both religious and cultural aspects and must be understood separately.

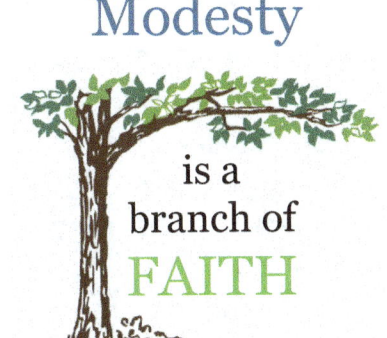

Modesty

is a branch of FAITH

- The Quran's guidance is the best for avoiding extremes.
- The opposite attribute is extravagance, show-off, boastfulness, pretense, speaking unnecessarily highly of yourself or someone/something, which God dislikes.
- Extravagance (and thus arrogance) creeps in slowly in individuals and in society, and people get immune to it.

## Three characteristics of a Muslim society

- Historically, every Muslim society always had these three distinguishing characteristics: Modesty, respect for elders, advising for the good, and forbidding the evil.
- They are primarily drawn from the religion of Islam, to the point that they have become part of the culture and entire civilization.
- Modesty is at the top of the list because it impacted even the cultures around Muslims.

**1** Modesty.

**2** Sense of respect for parents, elders, teachers, and relatives.

**3** Advising for the good and forbidding the evil.

# Modesty in Islam explained

- Modesty is a comprehensive term in Islam.
- It covers both inner and outer modesty.
- It's the inner modesty that is focused on, which creates the outer.
- Inner modesty is desired and is reflected in behavior, speech, appearance, and attitude toward people and toward God's directives.
- Inner modesty requires many things. Inner modesty should stop us from:

| Hadith |
| --- |
| If you feel no shame, then do whatever you like. (Sahih al-Bukhari) |

- Disobeying God without repenting.
- Arguing with our elders despite knowing that we are right.
- Dressing ourselves improperly, at any point in time, in any social setup.
- Always asking for something.
- Speaking ill of someone.

- Watching something that is not appropriate.
- Initiating, participating, or in any way. encouraging improper conversations (topics).
- Posting on social media something inappropriate.
- Drawing unnecessary attention to oneself.
- Mistreating others.

In today's world, wearing a hijab is considered modesty, which is just one aspect of modesty.

## Modesty defines levels of faith

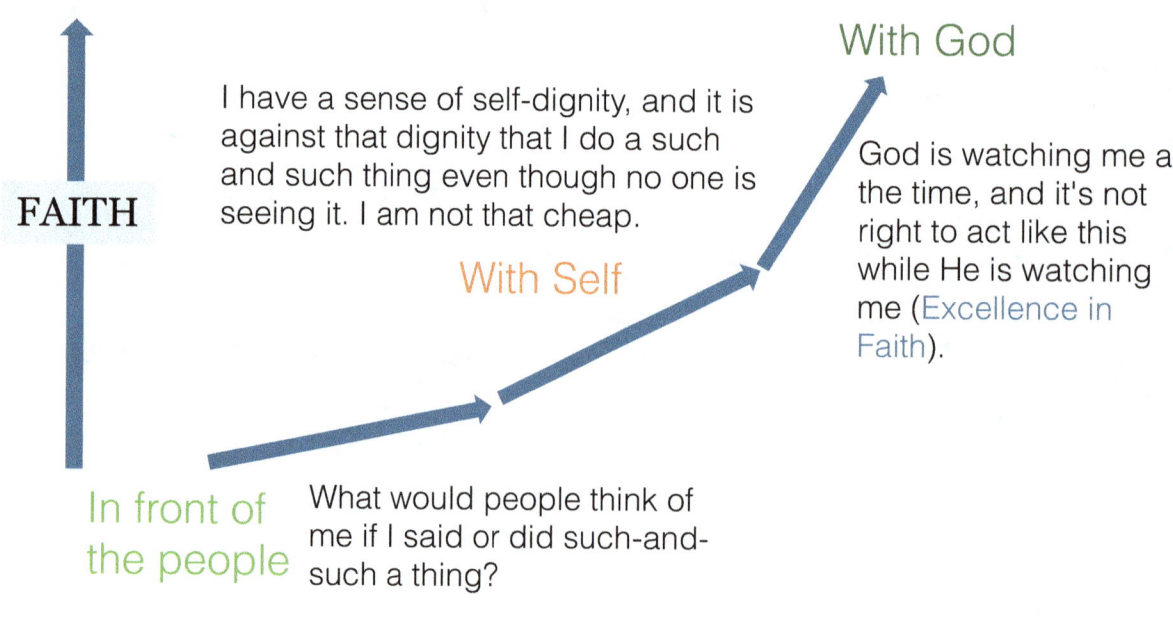

FAITH

With God

I have a sense of self-dignity, and it is against that dignity that I do a such and such thing even though no one is seeing it. I am not that cheap.

With Self

God is watching me all the time, and it's not right to act like this while He is watching me (Excellence in Faith).

In front of the people

What would people think of me if I said or did such-and-such a thing?

## Modesty in modern times

- Haya or modesty is an important trait of a believer, so it must transcend time and place.
- Its application may be different, but its essence cannot be lost.
- Haya should be seen as a huge part of your 'self-dignity.'
- Self-dignity acts as a barrier for you to say or do something inappropriate, not only in front of others but also when you are alone.
- 'Appropriate' should not be 'defined' by the Movies.
- Let Haya be our identity regardless of where we live.
- Haya is intrinsic in human personality, but societies condition themselves with time to act otherwise.
- Many societies were modest before, but now another human attribute has taken over: "freedom". In other words, it's not that people have lost the value of modesty, but rather they have preferred freedom over modesty.

Q? Were people more modest 100 years ago?

## Haya manifested in our appearance

- Although Haya is a broad term, in our society, Haya in appearance is important.
- Humans tend to go to extremes.
- What's 'mainstream' today was 'inappropriate' yesterday, and 'mainstream' yesterday was 'inappropriate' the day before ……………this is never-ending.
- Similarly, what's 'inappropriate' today WILL BE 'mainstream' tomorrow.
- The human-defined concept of modesty is relative with no 'standard'.
- God, in the Quran, gave us that criterion that should be adopted when dressing or behaving in public or in front of others who are not your family.
- It appears that women are expected to be more modest than men, but this is due to societal/cultural constructs that should not be our compass. Our only compass should be the Quran, which demands the same amount of modesty from both genders.
- If we say we 'believe' in God, pleasing 'others' goes against that belief.

Research: What was the concept of modesty for both men and women in the West 150-200 years ago, and how did people usually dress?

## Guidance from Quran

قُل لِّلْمُؤْمِنِينَ يَغُضُّوا مِنْ أَبْصَارِهِمْ وَيَحْفَظُوا فُرُوجَهُمْ ۚ ذَٰلِكَ أَزْكَىٰ لَهُمْ ۗ إِنَّ اللَّهَ خَبِيرٌ بِمَا يَصْنَعُونَ

وَقُل لِّلْمُؤْمِنَاتِ يَغْضُضْنَ مِنْ أَبْصَارِهِنَّ وَيَحْفَظْنَ فُرُوجَهُنَّ وَلَا يُبْدِينَ زِينَتَهُنَّ إِلَّا مَا ظَهَرَ مِنْهَا

وَلْيَضْرِبْنَ بِخُمُرِهِنَّ عَلَىٰ جُيُوبِهِنَّ

O Prophet, tell believing men to lower their gaze modestly and guard their chastity, it is purer for them, and God knows what they do. And similarly, tell believing women to lower their gaze modestly, guard their chastity, and not expose their adornments except what is usually revealed, and to cover their adornments by extending their head coverings to their collars/chest. (Quran 24:30-31)

## How to gain and maintain Haya

Modesty 'decay' is a process that goes through a long period of desensitization of society towards something that is 'inappropriate' before it becomes 'appropriate.'

- Be aware that God demands modesty from us, and it is tied to our faith.
- You 'define' for yourself what's appropriate and what's not appropriate in the light of the Quran and Sunnah – set your guidelines and apply them in your appearance and daily activities.
- 'Check' if you are getting desensitized to something that used to be 'inappropriate' for you.
- Find 'entertainment' for yourself, other than watching 'unlimited' TV.
- Pick your friends wisely.
- Spend some time with your elders at home.
- Adopt modesty as your 'identity' within your circle.
- Look for role models that embody modesty in all aspects.
- Remind yourself that God is watching even when you are alone.
- Make dua for guidance.

### Discussion Points

- Modesty and shyness are sometimes used interchangeably, but they are not the same!
- You can be bold and modest at the same time.
- Be modest in areas that hurt your self-dignity
- Modesty does not mean that you lose your 'confidence.'

## Adorn yourself with Haya in …..

- What you say
- What you watch
- What you read
- What you do
- What you wear
- How you treat others
- The way you address elders
- The places you go
- Choosing friends

## Guidance from Quran and Prophet's Best Example

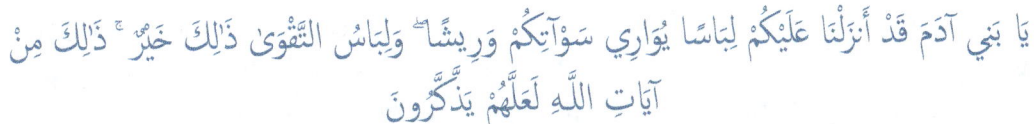

O children of Adam, we have given you clothing (dress) so that you can cover your body properly and adorn yourself from it, but the garment of righteousness is best for you. It is one of God's signs so that you remember. (Quran 7:26)

Every religion has a distinctive character. The character of Islam is modesty. (Hadith: Muwatta 47.2.9)

The Prophet passed by a man admonishing his brother about Haya, saying, "You are very shy, and I am afraid that might harm you." On that, Prophet Muhammad said, "Leave him, for Haya, is a part of Faith." (Hadith: Sahih Bukhari 73/139)

The Prophet was lying down in his house with his thighs exposed. Abu Bakr asked permission to enter, which was granted while the Prophet was in that position, and he came in and spoke with him. Then Umar asked permission to enter. He was granted permission to come in and speak with him while in that position. Then Uthman asked permission, and the Prophet sat up and straightened his clothing. He was then permitted to come in and speak with the Prophet. After he had gone, Aishah, his wife, said, "Abu Bakr entered, and you did not get up for him or worry about him, and Umar came in, and you did not get up for him nor worry about him, but when Uthman came in, you straightened out your clothing!" The Prophet said, "Should I not be shy of a man around whom the angels are shy?" (Hadith: Sahih Muslim)

## Quick Recap

- Haya is more than just how to dress and act in front of the opposite gender.
- The opposite attribute is boastfulness, which God dislikes.
- Shamelessness creeps in slowly in individuals and in society, and people get immune to it.
- Historically, Muslim societies have always had three distinguishing traits, and modesty is one of them.
- Modesty is both inner and outer. Inner modesty is desired and is reflected in behavior, speech, appearance, and attitude toward people and toward God's directives.
- Modesty should be from people, the self, and God, and that is the best of faith.
- Let Haya be our identity regardless of where we live.
- 'Check' if you are getting desensitized to something that used to be 'inappropriate' for you.

- Do you agree that peer pressure encourages or discourages modesty?
- Is it true from your experience that people from other faiths (the practicing ones) also promote modesty? Discuss examples.

# Chapter 20

# Respect

This chapter covers the concept of respect in Islam. This is one of those qualities that many societies have lost, but Islam teaches us that respect builds a beautiful culture and society.

# The concept of Respect

- Generally defined as a feeling of deep admiration for someone or something produced by their abilities, qualities, achievements, or association.
- Like other virtues in Islam, respect is a broader concept and is related to the following:
  - God
  - Human Beings
  - Objects/Things
- It is an integral part of Islam, and of the moral character it seeks to build.
- God has honored and dignified everyone and everything; so should we.

وَلَقَدْ كَرَّمْنَا بَنِي آدَمَ وَحَمَلْنَاهُمْ فِي الْبَرِّ وَالْبَحْرِ وَرَزَقْنَاهُم مِّنَ الطَّيِّبَاتِ وَفَضَّلْنَاهُمْ عَلَىٰ كَثِيرٍ مِّمَّنْ خَلَقْنَا تَفْضِيلًا

And We have dignified and honored the Children of Adam and given them means on the land and in the ocean, and given them provisions from pure things, and We gave them preference over many of Our creations. (Quran 17:70)

## REMINDER: Three characteristics of a Muslim society

- Historically, every Muslim society always had these three distinguishing characteristics: Modesty, **respect for elders**, advising for the good, and forbidding the evil.
- They are primarily drawn from the religion of Islam, to the point that they have become part of the culture and entire civilization.
- Respect for elders means to treat people according to your relationship with them. Your teacher and friend can't be treated the same way.

**1** Modesty.

**2** Sense of respect for parents, elders, teachers, and relatives.

**3** Advising for the good and forbidding the evil.

# Respect ....

**GOD**
Obeying Him

**Self**
Improving your image in the sight of God

**Parents**
Obeying them and listening to them

**Time**
Being punctual and not wasting it

**Others**
Giving them space and time

**Teachers**
Listening to them and thanking them

**Places**
Following the etiquettes

**Friends**
Being sincere with them

**Beliefs**
Not making fun of them

**Elders**
Behaving with manners

**Ideas**
Paying attention to them

**Religious Personalities**
Not mocking or making fun of them

**Religious Symbols**
Not mocking or making fun of them and following the etiquette

**Blessings**
Not wasting them

## Respect yourself

- Self-respect or self-esteem is equally stressed without crossing the line of vanity.
- Our 'image' before others should not consume us or lead to low self-respect.
- Every human being is born with talent and potential, and we should discover that.
- Know yourself to respect yourself.
- A lack of self-respect affects our personality and character development.
- Cherish who you 'are'.
- Let's judge ourselves in the sight of God.

يَا أَيُّهَا النَّاسُ إِنَّا خَلَقْنَاكُم مِّن ذَكَرٍ وَأُنثَىٰ وَجَعَلْنَاكُمْ شُعُوبًا وَقَبَائِلَ لِتَعَارَفُوا ۚ إِنَّ أَكْرَمَكُمْ عِندَ اللَّهِ أَتْقَاكُمْ ۚ إِنَّ اللَّهَ عَلِيمٌ خَبِيرٌ

O, people! We have created you from one man and one woman and made you tribes and clans so that you get to know one another. The noblest of you in God's sight is the most God-conscious. Indeed, God is all-knowing and wise. (Quran 49:13)

## Respect God by …

- Loving Him for everything that He has given us.
- Obeying His commands.
- Not disobeying Him by indulging in sins.
- Glorifying Him.
- Respecting His symbols – places of worship (mosques, churches), months (Ramadan), days (Eid), slaughtering animals, His Books etc.

**God is Self-Sufficient & All Creations Celebrate His Praises**

## Respect in relationships

- In relationships, respect is a two-way street, and this applies to all. For example, the elders must respect their younger to earn their respect.

YOU        OTHERS

- Among elders, parents are the most deserving of our respect.
- They provide us with so much, and in return, we MUST give them love and respect.
- We need to 'tune' our concept of respect as we grow up in Western society.
- Respect is most required when you do not agree with your parents or elders.
- Islam emphasizes respect for elders, whether they are relatives, teachers, mentors, friends, siblings, or neighbors.

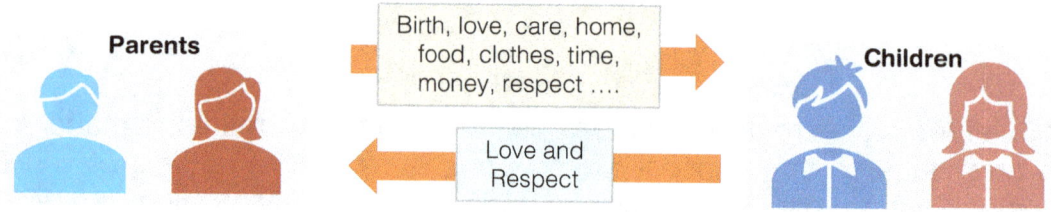

## Respecting teachers and mentors

- Teachers are people of knowledge, and the Quran grants them a special status.
- Respecting teachers and mentors is a lost virtue.
- They sacrifice their time and energy (time and energy they could have spent earning more) to shape our future.
- They complement our parents' role.
- Sometimes, we spend more time with our teachers than with our parents.
- They must be respected as much as our parents.

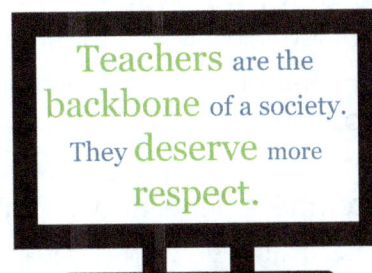

Teachers are the backbone of a society. They deserve more respect.

Students disrespecting their teachers are **NOT** cool.

## Respecting places of worship

- We should be utterly respectful of the places of worship for all religions.
- People have sentiments attached to them.
- Islam prohibits attacking places of worship, even during war.
- When visiting these places, including mosques, we should learn the etiquette to avoid being disrespectful.
- In Islamic countries, governments are responsible for protecting places of worship.

Mosque   Church
Monasteries   Synagogue

وَلَوْلَا دَفْعُ اللَّهِ النَّاسَ بَعْضَهُم بِبَعْضٍ لَّهُدِّمَتْ صَوَامِعُ وَبِيَعٌ وَصَلَوَاتٌ وَمَسَاجِدُ يُذْكَرُ فِيهَا اسْمُ اللَّهِ كَثِيرًا

And had it not been that Allah removed (counter) one people through another, the monasteries and churches, the synagogues, and the mosques, in which His praise is abundantly celebrated, would be utterly destroyed. (Quran 22:40)

Discuss some etiquette for mosques?

## Respecting others' ideas and opinions

- No "my way or the highway" attitude when discussing this with others.
- Human beings are not robots, so differences of opinion are natural.
- It is a test from God to deal with people of different temperaments and thoughts with respect.
- Learn to live with differences of opinion while remaining respectful.
- Humility and humbleness help respect others' opinions.

## Learn to respect

### Tolerance
We are going to face 'conflict' our entire life. Respect allows us to resolve the conflict in the best possible way.

### Listening
This is an essential part of having a productive conversation. Respecting others helps us listen without interrupting.

### Diversity
We should not make snap judgments about people without getting to know them. Learning to respect diversity allows us to give others the time and space they deserve.

### Basic Manners
Being respectful to others is a good starting point for developing basic manners. Respect provides us with the foundation for positive relationships with people.

## Guidance from Prophet's Best Example

Those who do not show mercy to our young ones and do not recognize the rights of our elders (by respecting them) are not from us. (Hadith: Musnad Ahmad 7033)

Prophet Muhammad was sitting with his companions when a funeral procession passed them, so he stood up. The companions said, 'O Prophet of Allah, it is the funeral procession of a Jew.' He said: 'Is it not a human soul?' (Hadith: Al-Bukhari and Muslim)

A delegation of around 60 Christians, headed by a bishop, once visited Prophet Muhammad in Medina. Prophet Muhammad hosted them in the mosque. While they were discussing matters with Prophet Muhammad, the time for their prayers approached, and they requested to pray. While honoring his guests, Prophet Muhammad permitted them to pray in the mosque however they wanted to. Prophet Muhammad respected their religion (knowing that they were on the wrong path) and their religious practices. (Source: Seerah)

Anas, a companion of Prophet Muhammad, said that one day Prophet Muhammad was sitting with us when a beautiful, handsome, rich, and famous man passed by. Prophet Muhammad asked, 'What do you say about this person?' They said he was excellent; if he spoke, everyone listened; if he interceded on someone's behalf, it would be granted; and if he proposed to any girl for marriage, he could marry that girl. Prophet Muhammad said, OK. Then, a poor and lowly man walked by. Prophet Muhammad asked, 'What do you say about this person?' They said no one cared what he had to say, so no one would listen to him; he wouldn't be able to intercede for anyone; and no one would give him their daughter in marriage. Prophet Muhammad said that the example/value of this person in the sight of God is better than the whole of the earth's example/value of that rich person. (Seerah of the Prophet)

Whenever Prophet Muhammad addressed someone with low self-respect or self-esteem, he mentioned their 'image' in God's sight.

## Quick Recap

- Respect is a broader concept related to God, people, and things.
- God has honored and dignified everyone and everything; so should we.
- Our 'image' before others should not consume us or lead to low self-respect.
- Let's judge ourselves in the sight of God.
- Respect God by not disobeying Him by being involved in sins.
- Respect is a two-way street in relationships.
- Respect is most required when you do not agree with your parents or elders.
- Teachers are the backbone of society, and they deserve more respect.
- When visiting places of worship, we should learn the etiquette to avoid being disrespectful.
- It is a test from God to deal with people of different temperaments and thoughts with respect.
- Whenever Prophet Muhammad addressed someone with low self-respect or self-esteem, he mentioned their 'image' in God's sight.

- How do movies affect our relationship with our parents and elders in terms of respect?
- How can remaining quiet help you learn respect for others?

# Chapter 21

# Keeping Promise

This chapter covers the concept of keeping promises or adhering to a contract in Islam. This is one of the most overlooked qualities of our society, which we sometimes don't even fully realize.

# The concept of keeping promises

"I will keep the trash outside after dinner."

"Don't you worry, I will take care of it."

"Yes, Insha'Allah, I will be there at 6 pm."

"Don't be so mean, I will return it tomorrow."

"Just give me a minute, and I will vacuum."

"No big deal, I can do it."

- The simple concept of keeping or fulfilling one's promise is to do what one said one would definitely do.
- Most of us take it very lightly.
- Fulfilling a formal contract is the ultimate way to keep a promise.
- Consistently keeping promises develops trustworthiness.
- Not keeping our promises is disrespectful to others and ourselves – it can hurt our self-esteem and our image before others (including God).

## Importance of fulfilling promises

- Breaking a promise is a great sin depending on the impact of it.
- Muslims are asked to keep their promises.
- Muslim nations must not break any treaty contracted with another nation.
- In Surah Tawbah, God announced punishment for those who deliberately rejected Prophet Muhammad as a messenger. Prophet was asked to declare all pacts and treaties null and void; however, it is explicitly stated that all time-limited treaties must continue until their terms expire.
- God repeated this statement multiple times in the Quran.

This is God's promise, and God never goes back on His promise, yet most men do not know it.

## Keeping promises promotes trust

- Trust plays a far-reaching role in our social affairs.
- Societies that lack trust in social affairs are broken from within.
- Keeping a promise or contract is one way to build that trust.
- Building trust is a gradual process – don't take any of your promises lightly.
- Promising habitually must be avoided.
- Be very clear when promising.
- Remember the old saying, "first impression is the last impression."

## Signs of a Hypocrite

There are four characteristics: whoever has them all is a pure hypocrite; when he speaks, he lies; when **he makes a promise, he breaks it; when he makes a covenant, he betrays it**; and when he disputes, he resorts to obscene speech. Whoever has one of them has one of the characteristics of hypocrisy until he gives it up. (Hadith: Bukhari 3178, Muslim 58)

**Note:** Prophet said that about the hypocrites of Medina.

## Guidance from the Quran

- The importance of keeping promises or adhering to the contract can be seen from these verses of the Quran:

وَأَوْفُوا بِالْعَهْدِ ۖ إِنَّ الْعَهْدَ كَانَ مَسْئُولً

Fulfill your promise/contract because it will be asked about. (Quran 17:34)

الَّذِينَ يُوفُونَ بِعَهْدِ اللَّهِ وَلَا يَنقُضُونَ الْمِيثَاقَ

Those who fulfill the covenant of Allah and do not break the contract. (Quran 13:20)

بَلَىٰ مَنْ أَوْفَىٰ بِعَهْدِهِ وَاتَّقَىٰ فَإِنَّ اللَّهَ يُحِبُّ الْمُتَّقِينَ

(And why not), Whosoever fulfills the covenant with God and is conscious of Him, then Allah loves those righteous people. (Quran 3:76)

يَا أَيُّهَا الَّذِينَ آمَنُوا أَوْفُوا بِالْعُقُودِ

O believers, fulfill your contracts and promises. (Quran 5:1)

## Punctuality – a promise fulfilled

- Being on time is not a favor to others. Its your responsibility.
- Respect your time and others' time.
- Most people DO NOT see it as a commitment.
- Being punctual or late becomes a habit easily if you strictly follow it.
- Being punctual is considered the trait of 'boring' people.
- Punctuality pays back in ways you can never imagine.
- It saves you from difficulties that you have never thought of.

## Avoid false promises – learn how to say NO

- The worst promise is the one that is made with the intention of not fulfilling it – It's a LIE.
- A false promise or a lie requires one to repent and compensate, as it is a sin.
- Say 'Insha'Allah' when promising to fulfill it.
- When making a promise to God, be very careful, as it will be asked of you on the day of judgment.
- Avoid promises when you are very happy or very sad
- Learn to say NO.
- It is OK to hurt someone's feelings on the spot and then make a false promise that you won't fulfill.

## Guidance from Prophet's Best Example

Whoever breaks the covenant of a Muslim, upon him be the curse of Allah, the angels, and all the people, and Allah will not accept any obligatory or voluntary act of worship from him." (Sahih al-Bukhari 1870, Muslim, 1370)

Allah will set up a banner for the betrayer on the Day of Resurrection, and it will be said: This is the betrayer of so and so." (Sahih al-Bukhari 6178, Muslim, 1735)

On the day of Hudaibiya, Prophet Muhammad made a peace treaty with non-Muslim tribes on three conditions. One of them was that Prophet Muhammad would return to them any person who flees to Prophet Muhammad (Even if this person converted to Islam). After the treaty, Abu Jandal Ibn Suhayl escaped from Makkah to Medinah. He was caught and came hoping to stay in Medinah, his legs being chained, but the Prophet returned him to the Mushrikeen due to the pact. (Seerah)

Hudhaifa bin Yaman did not participate in the Battle of Badr because of this incident. He narrated that he came out with my father Husail to participate in the battle, but the disbelievers of the Quraish tribe caught them. They asked: Do you intend to go to Muhammad? They said: "We do not intend to go to him, but we wish to go (back) to Medina." So they took from them a covenant in the name of God that they would turn back to Medina and would not fight on the side of Muhammad. So, they came to the Prophet and related the incident to him. The Prophet said: Both of you proceed (to Medina); we will fulfill the covenant made with them and seek God's help against them." (Seerah)

## Quick Recap

- Fulfilling a formal contract is the ultimate way to keep a promise.
- Consistently keeping promises develops trustworthiness.
- Muslim nations must not break any treaty contracted with another nation.
- Societies that lack trust in social affairs are broken from within.
- Remember the old saying, "first impression is the last impression."
- Respect your time and others' time.
- Punctuality pays back in ways you can never imagine.
- Avoid promises when you are very happy or very sad.
- Learn to say NO.

- What should I do if I can't keep my promise?
- How can I become more punctual?

# Chapter 22

# Habits

This chapter discusses the concept of habits and how habits can sometime destroy someone's personality even if they are good in nature.

# The concept of habit

Habit is stronger than nature.

**Quintus Curtius Rufus**

We are what we repeatedly do. Excellence, then, is not an act but a habit.

**Aristotle**

Adolescents become bound by the habits they create.
**(Dr. Carl E. Pickhardt, Ph. D.)**

- Habit is a routine of behavior that is repeated regularly and tends to occur subconsciously.
- A habit can be developed through support and repetition.
- It is so powerful that it can overcome someone's nature so be careful when developing habits.
- What we develop as habits during childhood shapes much of how we will behave as adults.
- Good habits are self-enhancing (you become better), and bad habits are self-defeating (you go down more).
- We are creatures of habits.
- We have 'free will', but our 'decision-making' is mostly driven by our habits.

## The role of habits in moral development

- Make the virtues that you learned in this course part of your personality.
- Use habits as a tool to build your moral character.
- Identify virtues that you think you need to work on or the ones that bring more joy when you act on them.
- Start with short and easy goals.
- One virtue leads to the other.
- Practice the virtue, not just appreciate it.
- We are not becoming angels.
- Worship is not a virtue; it only helps you do what you are supposed to do.
- A "charger" recharges your smartphone so you can use it to communicate.
- Same way the worship like Salah must recharges you to do good when you get our of your Salah.
- Salah should be more beneficial outside of Salah than inside Salah.

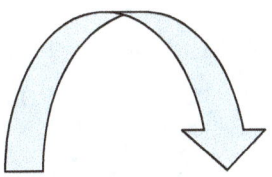

We are what we repeatedly do

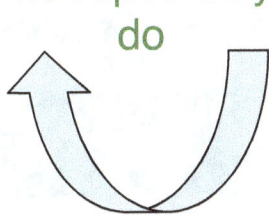

## Good habits and morals

### Truthfulness

- ✓ Agree with your parents that if you tell the truth, they will not punish you.
- ✓ Start telling the truth in situations that can put you in trouble.
- ✓ Don't lie even when joking.
- ✓ Listen more than talk.
- ✓ Stay on the topic that is being discussed.
- ✓ Avoid things/actions you don't want your parents to know.

### Humility

- ✓ Spend 5 minutes before bed reflecting on what you did wrong today.
- ✓ Pay attention to what's been said, not who said it.
- ✓ Don't make a quick judgment.
- ✓ Ask for forgiveness personally or forgive someone.
- ✓ Ask for advice from other people.
- ✓ Do not center the discussion around you.
- ✓ When you get a blessing, be grateful to God.

### Gratitude

- ✓ Count your blessings.
- ✓ Attribute every blessing to God.
- ✓ Make a habit of saying AlhamduLillah every time you eat or get some blessing.
- ✓ Be friends with people who are less fortunate than you.
- ✓ Share food with your neighbors or friends once a month.
- ✓ Donate $1 every Friday to a noble cause.
- ✓ Stop complaining.

**Pray five times, read a few verses from the Quran daily, attend Friday Khutbah, short talks, and make dua.**

# Bad Habits

## Effects of bad habits

- We are reward-based creatures – we prefer immediate reward.
- Bad habits make us feel good.
- Habits that go against our morality make a big sin look small.
- A habitual sin has a more powerful impact on our character than an occasional sin.
- A habitual sin puts us in a state of denial, and we find justifications easily.
- Bad habits pull us away from our goal of being a moral person.

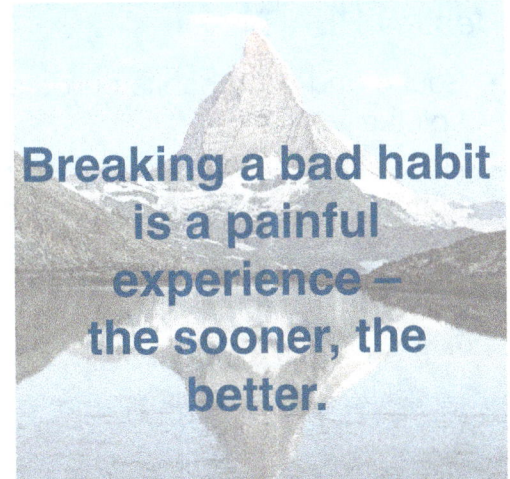

**Breaking a bad habit is a painful experience – the sooner, the better.**

**We cannot change something if we don't accept that something has to**

## Fixing bad habits

- Fixing bad habits is a slow and painful process and requires a lot of training and patience.
- It's an intentional process that you have to start and adopt. No one can do it for you. Of course, other people can help.

| | |
|---|---|
| **1** Identify and admit the bad habit. | **2** Make a sincere intention to get rid of this. |
| **3** Identify situations that trigger it and be vigilant. | **4** Immediately substitute it with a good habit. |
| **5** Remind yourself, out loud, that you want to get rid of this habit. | **6** Remember that every second of your effort is rewarded with good deeds. |
| **7** Don't get discouraged if you fail the first few times. Intention is rewarded. | **8** Immediately repent if you commit the mistake again. |
| **9** Change the company if you feel that people around you are not supportive. | **10** Make dua to God that He help you become a better person. |

# Guidance from the Quran and the Prophet's Best Example.

## Healthy HEART

- Sound and good habits builds a healthy heart both physiologically and spiritually.
- However, Allah wants us to see Him with sound and pure heart with no stain from evil thoughts, actions and habits.

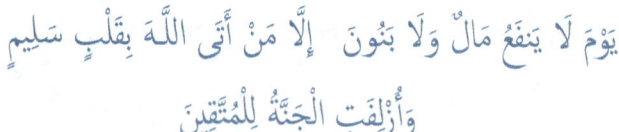

يَوْمَ لَا يَنفَعُ مَالٌ وَلَا بَنُونَ ۝ إِلَّا مَنْ أَتَى اللَّهَ بِقَلْبٍ سَلِيمٍ

وَأُزْلِفَتِ الْجَنَّةُ لِلْمُتَّقِينَ

The day when neither wealth nor children will help, but who will come with a **sound heart** (will be successful), and paradise will be brought closer to the ones who fear God. (Quran 26:88-90)

Truly, in the body is a piece of flesh which, if it is healthy, all the body is healthy and, if it is diseased, all of it is diseased. Truly, it is the heart." (Hadith: Bukhari and Muslim)

When the son of Adam wakes up in the morning, all of his limbs humble themselves to the **tongue,** and they say: "Fear Allah regarding us, for we are only a part of you. If you are upright, we are upright. If you are crooked, we are crooked." (Hadith: Sunan al-Tirmidhi 2407)

He who believes in Allah and the Last Day must either **speak** well or remain silent. (Hadith: Sahih Muslim)

Abu Musa Al-Ashari asked the Prophet: "Who is the most excellent among the Muslims?" He said, "One from whose **tongue** and hands the other Muslims are secure." (Hadith: Al-Bukhari and Muslim)

Whosoever gives me a guarantee to safeguard what is **between his jaws** and what is between his legs (private parts), I shall guarantee him Jannah. (Hadith: Sahih Al-Bukhari)

A person **utters a word** thoughtlessly (i.e., without thinking about its being good or bad) and, as a result of this, he will fall into the fire of Hell deeper than the distance between the east and the west. (Hadith: Sahih Bukhari and Muslim)

The Prophet said: "Do you know what backbiting is?" The Companions said: "Allah and His Messenger know better." He said, "Backbiting is talking about your (Muslim) brother in a manner that he would dislike." Someone said, "What if my (Muslim) brother is as I say?" He said, "If he is actually as you say, then **that is backbiting**; but if he is not as you say, then that is slandering. (Hadith: Sahih Muslim)

## Quick Recap

- We have 'free will', but our 'decision-making' is mostly driven by our habits.
- Habits can either pull you away from building your character or help you do that.
- Use the habit-building technique to make some virtues part of your personality.
- Bad habits are painful to get rid of; no slow-going about it.
- We cannot change something if we don't accept that something has to change.
- Worship is not a virtue; it only helps you do what you are supposed to do.
- The heart is at the center of our personality – we must work on our hearts.
- Our tongue is the source of most of our moral challenges.

- Identify a bad habit and how you plan to get rid of it. Share it with your teacher only (like an assignment).
- Identify a good habit you want to build as part of your personality and tell everyone why you picked that habit and how you will achieve that goal.

# Chapter 23

# Dealing with Life Situations

In this chapter, a list of real-life situations are given to test you how do you apply your knowledge of the course in addressing those situations.

# Life Scenarios

Based on what you have learned in this course, apply your knowledge in these scenarios and discuss what would you do:

**Situation 1:** I belong to a lower-middle-class family, and I don't have many of the things some of my friends have.

**Situation 2:** I am in a situation where I need to mete out justice to someone I despise.

**Situation 3:** Some children don't like me, and I must turn them into friends.

**Situation 4:** I want to be non-judgmental when dealing with someone whom I know has a bad reputation.

**Situation 5:** Someone hit me hard, and I am mad.

**Situation 6:** I just learned that my good friend, who is living with his uncle, is sick while his parents are visiting their parents in another city.

**Situation 7:** I am new to a school and looking for new friends.

**Situation 8:** I got $500 for my birthday and want to spend it.

**Situation 9:** My younger brother is annoying my mom while she is cooking dinner.

**Situation 10:** I did not get good grades this year, but my friend did.

**Situation 11:** I got detention in school, and my mom asked me what happened.

**Situation 12:** I hurt my friend's feelings, and he/she is mad.

**Situation 13:** Someone sent me a message saying my friend did something really bad, and they want me to forward it to everyone so everyone knows.

**Situation 14:** My friend sometimes steals things in school, and I have to do something about it.

**Situation 15:** I am embarrassed that all of my friends have the new iPhone while I am still using the older model.

**Situation 16:** I cannot believe I just found $20 on the floor at school.

**Situation 17:** My grandmother is visiting us this weekend, but my friends want me to spend time with them.

**Situation 18:** My mom is angry at something, and she shouted at me, and I did not like it at all.

# Life Scenarios

Based on what you have learned in this course, apply your knowledge in these scenarios and discuss what would you do:

**Situation 19:** I noticed that, as I try to be a good person, develop good habits, and give up bad ones, I am not as popular at my school anymore.

**Situation 20:** My friend told me to tell his mother something different than what happened (basically a lie) so he does not get in trouble.

**Situation 21:** You know that your team cheated in the game, but no one saw, so your teammates decided to stay quiet.

**Situation 22:** I am in the middle of playing a video game and on the last level, and my sister told me that our aunt came to visit us and she is downstairs.

**Situation 23:** I have some savings this year, and Eid is approaching. I can afford a couple of gifts and am wondering who I should give them to.

**Situation 24:** I usually get harmful posts from my friends in a chat group, and I keep deleting them.

**Situation 25:** We were debating about something at a family gathering, and my cousin insulted me during the argument.